WALKS THROUGH

Marie Antoinette's

Paris

DIANA REID HAIG

RAVENHALL BOOKS

Walks Through Marie Antoinette's Paris
First published 2006 by Ravenhall Books, an imprint of Linden Publishing l.imited

© Diana Reid Haig, 2006

Cover illustration: Equestrian portrait of Queen Marie Antoinette in hunting costume, 1783. Louis Auguste Brun de Versoix.
Illustration on p. 7: Marie Antoinette of Austria, Dauphine of France, 1773. After François-Hubert Drouais.

British Library Cataloguing in Publication Data
Haig, Diana Reid
Walks through Marie Antoinette's Paris
l.Marie Antoinette, Queen, consort of Louis XVI, King of France, 1755-1793 - Homes and haunts - France - Paris
2.Walking - France - Paris - Guidebooks 3.Paris (France) History - 1715-1789 4.Paris (France) - Guidebooks
I.Title
914.4'361'0484
ISBN-10: 1905043082

Ravenhall Books, PO Box 357, Welwyn Garden City, AL6 6WJ, United Kingdom
www.ravenhallbooks.com

www.marieantoinettesparis.com

Tourist information contained in this book was accurate when it was published, but please confirm details before planning your trip.

Printed and bound in China by Compass Press.

TABLE OF CONTENTS

ACKNOWLEDGEMENTS

Photography/proofreading: Elliot Mazer
Proofreading/scanning: Guilio Dattero, Sarah Stafford
Topography advisor: Alison Mazer

A special thank you to Jonathan and Evgenia North at Ravenhall Books, Rachel Fox, Jérémie Benoit/Château de Versailles, and Estelle Dietrich/Musée de l'Histoire de France for access to Marie Antoinette's "dress book".

The author is grateful for the contributions of: Deborah Esposito, David Bell, Jacqueline Chambord, Florence Cavé, Selma Chibane, Kristina Czerniachowicz/French Institute-Alliance Française, Denis Bruckman/Bibliothèque Nationale, Catherine Jenkins, Elizabeth Zanis, Deanna Cross, Rebecca Akan/Metropolitan Museum of Art, Emmanuel Breguet, Franciane Guibert, Aurelie Hugon/Breguet, François Mellerio, Diane-Sophie de Raigniac, Jean-Loup Giriat/Mellerio dits Meller, Claudette Blackwood/Bernadaud-Royale, Bernard Poisson/Debauve & Gallais, Marion Fourestier/French Government Tourism Office, Norman Barth/Paris.org, Paula Prezioso, Denise Seidelman, Nina Rumbold, Dawn Smith-Pliner, Mary Walsh Snyder and FIA, Adam Sohmer, Jeanne Solomon, Holly Gleason, Nancy and Larry Price, Connie and Bill Nichols, Will Jennings, Monika Stafford, Peter Hicks, Glenn Durbin, Marshall Chapman, Candice Nancel/US Embassy-Paris, Joseph Guarino, Robin and Bill Kallam, Richard DonDiego, Teddy Irwin, C. C. Couch, Guillaume Verzier, Beatrice Grima, Marie-Claude Chira, Olessia Voltchenkova/Prelle, Evelyn Placek, Shari Leipsiz, Ronald Freyberger, Joel Hellman, Susan Owens/Royal Collection at Windsor Castle,

Will Salmon, Dave Stefancic, Nicolas de La Morinière/Odiot, Douglas Allen, Philip Corso, Joy Thomas, David Markham, David Stefanic, Druanne Martin, Sonya Polonsky, Gilliam Greyson, Sarah Gilbert Fox and Stephanie Cajoleas, Stephanie Steele, Simone Lazer, Jully and Anna Vinasco, Ben Weider, Cindy Tracy/World of Reading, Julie Hart, Cara Haack/Teacher's Discovery, Susan Simmons and the staff at First Presbyterian CDC, Wayne Furman/New York Public Library, Reidsville Public Library, Rockingham County Public Library, Susan Benning/May Memorial Library, Michael Snodin/Victoria and Albert Museum, Becky Carrigan/Barnes & Noble, Shaun Dobbs/WH Smith, Hatchards, Galignani, Ryan Jensen/Art Resource, Melanie McGurr, Eileen Angelini, and Jennifer Appel.

Heartfelt thanks to the entire staff at Britthaven of Madison, especially Anne Skow, Jamie Aswell, Frances DeChurch, Lynn Moore, Phyllis Hames, Adrienne Schultz, Vicky Tinsley, Kaneesha Glover, Betty Stevens, Susan Corns, Kay Skow, Sue Vaughn, Yvonne Hawkins, Beverley Alverson, Nancy Willis, Regina Mulloy, Becky Conway, Telisa Lowe, Rose Bean, Judy Jeffries, Donna Vaughn, Tammy Neal, Barbara Dishman, Shannon Knight, Linda Wood, Angie Broadnax, Robin Blott, Annette Hopper, Gladys Nowlin, Trisha Bullins, Melanie Murphy, Natalie Barrett, Mike Barber, Roy Malasco, Olivia Holly, Kelly Goins, Robert Pettigrew, and Earl Dawson.

Visit www.marieantoinettesparis.com

for Jack, my chou d'amour, *for my mother,*
Diana Thompson, who first showed me France,
and for my father, Martin Haig, who loves words

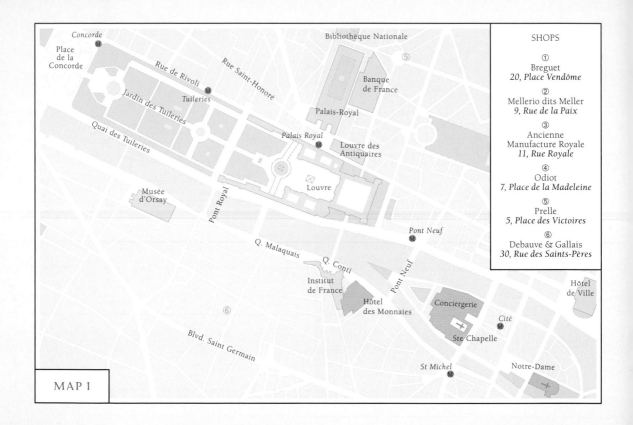

Concorde

Place
de la
Concorde

Rue de Rivoli

Rue Saint-Honoré

Jardin des Tuileries

Tuileries

Quai des Tuileries

Musée
d'Orsay

Pont Royal

Bibliothèque Nationale

Banque
de France

Palais-Royal

Palais Royal

Louvre des
Antiquaires

Louvre

Q. Malaquais

Q. Conti

Institut
de France

Hôtel
des Monnaies

Pont Neuf

Pont Neuf

Blvd. Saint Germain

Conciergerie

Ste Chapelle

Hôtel
de Ville

Cité

St Michel

Notre-Dame

MAP 1

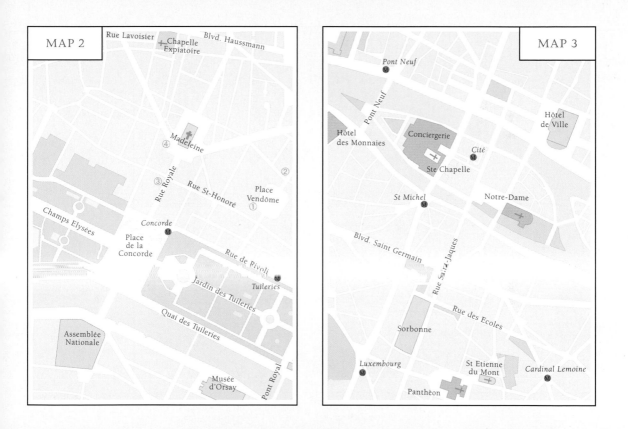

CHÂTEAU DE COMPIÈGNE.

Collection of the author.

CHÂTEAU DE COMPIÈGNE

MAY 14, 1770. ON A SUNNY SPRING AFTERNOON, TRUMPETS AND DRUMS ECHOED THROUGH THE THICK GREEN FOREST NEAR COMPIÈGNE, A ROYAL CHÂTEAU 40 MILES NORTHEAST OF PARIS. An elaborate cortège of 48 sumptuous coaches, each pulled by a team of six horses, wound its way slowly along the road. At the centre of the procession, tucked inside a new golden carriage of jewel-like perfection sat a petite, blooming 14-year-old blonde: the living symbol of a political alliance made in 1756 between traditional enemies France and Austria. The marriage of Archduchess Marie Antoinette – spoiled youngest daughter and fifteenth child of the great Austrian empress Maria Theresa – with the Dauphin Louis-Auguste, heir to the French throne, linked these two nations for the first time. This new marital bond astonished the people of both countries who despised each other – a result of centuries of warfare between the Austrian Hapsburgs and the French Bourbons.

Magnificently dressed in the latest Parisian fashion, the small girl looked like a life-size doll in her voluminous silk gown, edged with yards of fine lace. She knew her fatiguing three-week journey from Vienna to Versailles was nearing its end. Today she would meet her husband. Although she had been married by proxy before she left Vienna, Marie Antoinette had only seen her bridegroom in portraits.

As she rode in the ornate carriage with its crimson velvet upholstery, she sometimes looked at miniatures of her family, the only remaining souvenirs from her life in Vienna. From the moment she entered her new country, etiquette demanded that all possessions brought with her be discarded. Everything she owned must now be French; she was given new clothes, shoes and jewellery. Even her name was changed from Maria Antonia to the Gallic Marie

LOUIS-AUGUSTE IN 1769 (BY LOUIS-MICHEL VAN LOO) AND MARIE ANTOINETTE IN 1770 (BY JEAN-BAPTISTE CHARPENTIER).

akg-images

Antoinette. Strangers replaced the familiar Austrian ladies. Her new First Lady-in-Waiting, the humourless Comtesse de Noailles, sat beside her in the coach instructing her on the intricate etiquette used at the Bourbon court.

Nearby, Louis XV, cheerfully dissolute at 60 but still handsome, stood beneath the massive oaks and chestnuts on the edge of the forest waiting impatiently to meet his grandson's wife. He had travelled from Versailles to welcome the new Dauphine and was visibly more excited than the bridegroom, a tall sullen boy of 16.

Behind rows of French Guards in their bright blue coats, local townspeople gathered to catch a glimpse of their future queen. Finally, the first outriders galloped into sight announcing the procession's approach. Soon the forest was filled with the sound of wheels, the cracking of postilions' whips and the neighing of horses. A long line of carriages appeared and in another moment, Marie Antoinette's ornate coach, its roof decorated by flowers carved in gold with coloured enamelled petals, came into view. Enthusiastic shouts greeted her arrival.

A small head with pink cheeks and ash-blonde hair arranged in curls peeped out of the open left-hand window and spied the king. The procession halted. Marie Antoinette stepped down from the coach, paused for an instant, flashed a smile, then impetuously flew to Louis XV as fast as her silk-clad shoes and side-bustled gown would allow. She described the scene in a letter to her mother: "I saw a huge cortège. It was the king who had the goodness to come and surprise me. As soon as I saw him, I threw myself at his feet in great confusion. He took me in his arms, kissed me again and again, and called me his dear daughter with a kindness that would have touched my mama."

Louis XV, delighted by the blue-eyed innocent, gently lifted her up and gave her a long appraising glance. This connoisseur of women, whose sexual dalliances often included liaisons with prostitutes as young as his new granddaughter, then introduced Marie Antoinette to her husband. Louis-Auguste, as required by etiquette, kissed her on the cheek as the watching crowd clapped and cheered.

CHÂTEAU DE COMPIÈGNE

There has been a royal residence at Compiègne since the fourteenth century. In the mid-1700s, Louis XV decided to rebuild the castle, then a simple two-storey hunting lodge. He called upon Ange-Jacques Gabriel, a gifted, innovative architect who also designed the Petit Trianon at Versailles and Place Louis XV (now Place de la Concorde) in Paris. Gabriel renovated the château in a nascent austere style with elegant proportions that was eventually called Neoclassicism. Work on the palace was not completed when Marie Antoinette arrived in France. After her husband was crowned in 1774, this quickly became his favourite home, and he was severely criticized for the enormous sums he spent here. Of Marie Antoinette's rooms at Compiègne, only the Salon des jeux, *where she played cards in the evening, has been restored to its original splendour. The cool white panelling of this room was complimented by rich wall hangings decorated with green garlands and pink roses. The design was reconstructed from a swatch of the exact pattern made for Marie Antoinette in the mid-1780s; the original was made in Lyons by the Pernon firm, a manufacturer who supplied silk to many courts in the late 1700s.*

In 1782, after Marie Antoinette had given birth to the couple's first son, Louis XVI ordered that this château be completely refurbished. The queen asked to use a suite of rooms adjacent to the terrace on the right of the Cour Royale. Part of the terrace was sectioned off as a private area for the royal family, and Marie Antoinette loved to sit there with her children and gaze at the 2,000 lime trees surrounding the garden.

The national museum of the Château de Compiègne is open every day, except Tuesday, from 10.00 am to 6.00 pm (last admission at 5.15 pm). The Great Apartments are open from 10.00 am to 3.45 pm (last admission). Trains leave from Paris for Compiègne from the Gare du Nord.

The king, Louis-Auguste and Marie Antoinette rode back to Compiègne, where the bride was to spend her first night with the French royal family. The high-spirited girl chatted easily with the king in the back of the coach while her young husband brooded and looked in the other direction. As the carriages rolled into the front courtyard, dignitaries and courtiers lined up on the magnificent grand staircase to greet the bride.

Arriving at the château, used by Louis XV as a summer residence, Marie Antoinette was led to her apartment by the king and Dauphin, each holding one of her hands. In a salon resplendent with mirrors, the rest of the royal family waited to be presented. The bride made a good first impression upon the jaded courtiers. Jeanne Campan, who met Marie Antoinette at this time and later served as First Lady of the Bedchamber, remembered: "The Dauphine, beaming with freshness, appeared to all eyes more than beautiful... One could not help but admire the airy lightness of her walk. Her eyes were soft; her smile friendly... All who met her were charmed."

That night Marie Antoinette and her young husband ate in public beside the king in a vast salon decorated with costly Gobelins tapestries showing hunting scenes set in the nearby forest. When the exhausted girl finally returned to her rooms, the Grand Master of Ceremonies brought her a dozen golden wedding rings. She tried them on until one fit perfectly, and handed it to him for use in her upcoming religious wedding at Versailles in two days. Then her ladies undressed her and congratulated her upon completing her first day with the court, saying, "Madame, you delight everyone." Early the next morning the king and royal family left Compiègne on the last stage of the journey that would carry Marie Antoinette to Versailles, the sumptuous palace that served as the centre of French government.

Louis-Auguste did not stay with his bride but slept that night at a nearby mansion belonging to one of the king's ministers. Although the new husband kept a journal of his activities, all he jotted in his diary that momentous day in regards to the girl who would soon share his bed was the terse comment, "Meeting with Madame la Dauphine".

A VIEW OF THE CHAPEL AT VERSAILLES BY JEAN BAPTISTE RIGAUD.

CHÂTEAU DE VERSAILLES
ROYAL CHAPEL AND OPERA HOUSE

TWO DAYS AFTER MEETING HER BRIDEGROOM AT COMPIÈGNE, MARIE ANTOINETTE RODE THROUGH THE TALL DECORATIVE IRON GATES OF THE CHÂTEAU AT VERSAILLES FOR THE FIRST TIME. VERSAILLES, built in the 1600s by Louis XIV as a pleasure palace, looks very much the same today as when the new Dauphine's carriage stopped in the marble-paved front courtyard at 10.00 am on Wednesday 16 May 1770.

Peering out the window of her coach at the monumental palace, the largest in Europe, the young girl stared at the splendour of her new home. Her lady-in-waiting showed her the spires of the royal chapel, where her marriage was scheduled to begin in three hours. The enormous estate, which housed 5,000 courtiers, was bustling with last-minute preparations for the wedding. Excitement filled the air as the finest carpenters, gardeners and gilders in the realm rushed through the halls and grounds putting final touches on the decorations. To celebrate his grandson's marriage, the king had commissioned a new opera house on the east side of the château, and labourers hurried to complete this theatre where the wedding banquet would be held. The day was overcast, and everyone anxiously regarded the sky to see if the huge fireworks display scheduled for that evening would be cancelled.

There was no time for Marie Antoinette to tour the château with its grand state apartments – the definition of seventeenth-century French royal taste: exquisitely painted ceilings, lavish gilding and ornate doors. The 14-year-old bride was immediately whisked into ground-floor rooms where hairdressers, milliners and chambermaids set to work preparing her for the royal nuptials. The slim girl, who, according to observers, did not look older than 12, was laced into a tight whale-boned bodice, then dressed in a petticoat with *panniers*, large basket-shaped hoops rising up on each side of the hips. Her wedding gown was an extravagant white confection shimmering with threads of gold, silver and rose. Diamonds, sewn onto the front of the bodice, flashed with her every move. As seamstresses made frantic last-minute adjustments, the king arrived to introduce her to the Dauphin's two younger sisters: nine-year-old Clotilde and six-year-old Elisabeth. Marie Antoinette loved children and, to the dismay of her ladies, insisted on stopping her toilette to romp with little Elisabeth.

At 1.00 pm, she was led to the king's cabinet (*cabinet du Conseil*) where the royal family lined up and began the nuptial cortège through the halls and adjoining rooms of the *grands appartements*. The court's Grand Master of Ceremonies, stiff with grandeur in a brocade and lace suit, led the procession. Louis-Auguste, who had hardly spent a moment alone with Marie Antoinette during the last two days, took his bride's hand, and together they slowly walked towards the royal chapel. A page trailed behind the Dauphine carrying the heavy train of her dress.

The elite of France had been invited to the glittering occasion, and thousands of spectators jammed the salons and staircases. As this was Marie Antoinette's first appearance at Versailles, everyone was eager to see the Austrian Archduchess glide across the parquet floor on her way to the chapel. Tiers of seats filled the halls so that visitors could get a better view, and the crowd buzzed with expectation and conjecture.

The young girl's poise was remarkable. Observers admired her sparkling eyes and wonderful complexion and noticed that she beamed at the crowd while her husband, dressed in a costly golden suit, heavy with diamond-studded decorations, seemed ill at ease. The bride's lightheartedness and natural grace proved a marked contrast to the groom's scowl and clumsy gait, which sneering courtiers said resembled a waddle. Her husband's younger brothers, the duplicitous Comte de Provence (later Louis XVIII) who was the same age as Marie Antoinette, and the fun-loving Comte d'Artois (later Charles X), two years younger, marched behind the young couple. The rest of the royal family and 70 ladies of the court, in dazzling gowns and elaborate headdresses, followed them. An onlooker remembered, "Nothing could have exceeded the magnificence of the costumes." The king walked alone near the end of the cortège, and his imposing presence hushed the crowd. The brilliant procession passed through the long Hall of Mirrors, the most famous room in the palace, and wound its way through the state apartments.

When the young couple reached the stately chapel, built of pale white stone with clear glass windows that allowed sunlight to fill the room, the great organ began a crescendo of music. The spectators rose; when the king appeared, his red-coated Swiss Guards began to beat a rhythmic tattoo on their drums. The chapel was filled with the most important dignitaries in Europe, and women in delicate, shimmering silk, all competing to be best dressed. The ladies were crammed so tightly together that the hoop skirts of their new gowns were mashed and ruined. An observer, the Duc de Croÿ, was struck by their gorgeous jewellery and noted that "all one saw was a solid amphitheatre of fine clothes. Above all the sunlight brought out their brilliance."

Marie Antoinette and Louis-Auguste knelt on red velvet cushions at the steps of the high altar. The king, who usually watched the service from an upper gallery above the main entrance, remained near the young couple as the Archbishop of Rheims blessed the wedding rings and 13 gold pieces that represented the symbolic sale of the bride. Louis-Auguste repeatedly glanced at the king for approval, and the Duchess of Northumberland, an English noblewoman who received one of the 5,000 highly coveted invitations, commented, "The Dauphin appeared to have more timidity than his little wife. He trembled excessively during the service and blushed up to his eyes when he gave the [wedding] ring. When Mass began and they presented him with a book, he looked quite relieved to have an excuse for not looking about."

After the royal orchestra, seated behind the altar, performed a sacred cantata, the young couple stepped beneath a canopy of silver cloth while the archbishop completed the Mass. Then, according to custom, a priest from the town of Versailles handed the king the parish register where all local marriages were recorded. Louis XV signed with a flourish, followed by the Dauphin who wrote "Louis-Auguste" in a neat hand. Then the bride was given the pen, and the composure she showed during the interminable festivities vanished. As the royal family watched, Marie Antoinette slowly and laboriously scratched out her full name in a clumsy, crooked line and left a large black inkblot on the marriage contract. She even made two misspellings in her own name; her lack of education – she could barely read or write when she left Austria – suddenly became glaringly obvious.

Most of the guests enthusiastically praised the Dauphine, but she did not receive unanimously good reviews. The Duchess of Northumberland remembered that, despite the splendour of the bride's costume, her gown did not fit well. "Her robe was too small," wrote the duchess, "and left a broad stripe of lacing and shift quite visible, which had a bad effect between two broader stripes of diamonds. She really had quite a load of jewels…"

Finally, the nuptial procession returned to Louis XV's apartments, but there was no time for the bride to rest. Marie Antoinette hurried back to her rooms to receive the pledges of loyalty from the officers of her new staff. As *Madame la Dauphine* she now became head of her own household. Her personnel included 13 ladies, 14 waiting women, 19 valets, 18 lackeys, five *maîtres d'hôtel*, four surgeons, two doctors, a clock-maker, wig-maker and tapestry-maker. Although Marie Antoinette was a light eater and not easily tempted by epicurean delights, over 100 servants were employed solely to prepare her food.

Since the king's wife was dead, Marie Antoinette now became the highest-ranking female in France, and Louis XV presented the 14-year-old with the gems of the queens and Dauphines. The young girl, who loved lavish jewellery, could now wear magnificent diamonds once owned by Anne of Austria and others collected by Catherine de Médicis and Mary Queen of Scots. The king also showered her with extravagant personal gifts including a fan covered in jewels, an elegant blue enamel watch, and a necklace of pearls the size of small nuts. These treasures arrived in an ornate jewellery casket, six feet long and three and a half feet high, designed by the artist Belanger, who created the wedding invitations.

A huge reception began in the late afternoon, followed by the *Jeu du Roi*, a tradition that allowed the public, behind balustrades, to watch the royal family play cards. The king enjoyed his favourite game, lansquenet, seated at a small table covered by green velvet and with Marie Antoinette at his right. Massive chandeliers with hundreds of flickering candles lit the ornate rooms as more than 6,000 guests were ushered through the **grands appartements**. A sudden downpour caused the firework extravaganza in the park to be postponed and, in addition to the invited guests, the drenched spectators crowded into the château.

At 10.00 pm, it was time for the wedding banquet and the inauguration of the *Salle des Spectacles*, also called the *Opéra*. The courtiers, eager for their first glimpse of the new building, hurried to inspect and marvel at the details. Built by the king's favourite architect Gabriel, this theatre, made almost entirely of hand-carved wood either gilded or painted to resemble marble, was aesthetic perfection. Decorated by the leading sculptors and artists of the day and filled with brilliant blue silk and velvet upholstery, the opera house could seat a thousand guests. Its unusual design featured a novel trick: the floor of the stage could be raised or lowered so that, with the addition of a wooden platform over the orchestra pit and seats, the room could be used as a theatre, a ballroom or banquet room. For the wedding feast, a massive rectangular table sat in the middle of the room surrounded by thousands of candles. The king presided at the head of the table with the Dauphin and Dauphine on either side and the 25 members of the royal family seated

THE MARRIAGE OF THE DAUPHIN AND DAUPHINE
AT THE CHAPEL AT VERSAILLES.
Collection of the author.

according to precedence. A marble balustrade separated the royalty from the officials and courtiers, and these were allowed to watch the meal but were not served supper. Eighty members of the King's Orchestra sat at the back of the stage ready to perform during the feast. A drum-roll sounded, and the royal caterers and servants in colourful livery marched in carrying golden trays overflowing with hundreds of savoury delicacies from the palace kitchens.

For the first time that day, Louis-Auguste smiled and looked pleased. Irresistibly attracted to food, the Dauphin had been known to eat sweets and cake until he was sick. Although Marie Antoinette barely nibbled her dinner, the courtiers noted that Louis-Auguste ate as if famished and attacked his dinner with such a vengeance that the king leaned over and whispered, "Don't overeat tonight." The Dauphin paused, gave him a puzzled look, and replied, "Why not? I always sleep better after a good meal." The king glanced sadly at Marie Antoinette then gave a rueful smile.

Soon it was time for the evening's final event: the ritual of the royal couple's bedding. The Dauphin and Dauphine walked to their room as the bands of the Swiss and French Guard played a lively air. The most important courtiers watched as the Archbishop of Rheims blessed the bed and the newly married couple were handed their nightclothes. The Dauphin seemed sleepy and withdrawn while Marie Antoinette smiled engagingly at him. They climbed into bed; the room was filled with silence as the curtains were closed, then reopened to show the bride and groom in bed together. The court bowed and left the bedchamber. Louis-Auguste quickly fell asleep and snored loudly.

Marie Antoinette was bewildered by her husband's behaviour. She was not ignorant about sex and, before leaving Austria, had been told what to expect on her wedding night. She knew it was her duty to provide France with an heir, and her mother had emphasized that the future of the Austrian and French alliance hinged upon her marital success. Although the rest of her education had been ignored, the 14-year-old received elaborate instructions from the empress about the importance of pleasing the Dauphin. Maria Theresa, who had borne 16 children, taught her daughter that, "the woman must be completely submissive to her husband and have no other occupation than to please and obey him. The only real happiness in this world is a happy marriage… and the entire thing depends on the woman, if she is willing, gentle, and amusing."

Louis-Auguste was completely inexperienced with women, ignorant of the basic acts necessary to procreate, and may have suffered from a condition called phymosis, in which the foreskin of the penis cannot retract, making erection painful or impossible. He was shy and awkward; some felt this was because his parents died before he was a teenager. His interest in the opposite sex seemed almost nonexistent, and the king, who delighted in carnal pleasure, even wondered if his grandson was capable of fathering children. Referring to Louis-Auguste's virility, Louis XV commented, "He is not like other men."

The next morning most of Versailles knew the marriage had not been consummated. Not only had the pyrotechnics display celebrating the wedding been cancelled, there had been no fireworks between the bride and groom. Chambermaids working in the couple's bedroom acted as spies and reported on the status of the nuptial sheets. In his little grey diary, Louis-Auguste's entry for that day consisted of one word: "*rien*" (nothing). The next night the young couple seemed no closer to becoming intimate, and the Dauphin appeared almost oblivious to the pretty girl sleeping in his bed. He began to rise early in the morning to go hunting, leaving his bride asleep. The court buzzed with speculation: Couldn't the Dauphine excite the heir to the throne? What exactly was the problem? Marie Antoinette confided to her tutor, the Abbé de Vermond, that her husband had not kissed her or even held her hand.

She wrote to her mother, who quickly replied advising patience and added, "I cannot repeat it enough: no petulance: just caresses and cajoling. Too much eagerness could spoil everything… You are both so young…. It is all for the best. You will both gain strength." While her husband hunted, the homesick Dauphine sat alone playing with her beloved little dog, Mops, a miniature boxer that had been brought from Vienna.

For the next two weeks, Marie Antoinette was rushed from the opera to ballets, theatrical performances, and receptions. A ball was given in her honour in the new Opera House. The bride and groom danced a minuet to open the ball, with Louis-Auguste predictably stiff and embarrassed. Then the royal family joined in quadrilles and country-dances; the sprightly Dauphine was greatly admired. The same night, 19 May, 200,000 Parisians flocked to Versailles to celebrate the wedding. Acrobats and tightrope-walkers entertained to the sounds of orchestras spread throughout the gardens, illuminated with 90,000 lamps. The fireworks display was finally given. The royal family gathered in the Hall of Mirrors where the king threw a flaming spear from a window to signal the start of the pyrotechnics.

Almost 30,000 rockets exploded in the sky over Versailles. Patriotic emblems, such as golden revolving suns decorated with the French coat of arms and the Dauphin and Dauphine's initials, were incorporated in the fireworks. The royal family watched the dazzling show from the terrace. After the last Roman candle sputtered out, revellers danced in the gardens until dawn. Fireworks in Paris, held in the Place Louis XV (now Place de la Concorde) caused a stampede that left over 130 people dead. The expense was astronomical and further drained an already depleted French treasury. Many of the workmen were never paid, and Gabriel, who built the Opera, remarked that the builders at Versailles were "weighed down by the misery and debts which they incurred in the service of the king."

Throughout the celebrations, Marie Antoinette continued to charm the king and the court. "She is all smiles," remarked the Austrian ambassador to Paris. Despite the tremendous cost of the festivities, it was generally conceded that Louis-Auguste's wedding to Marie Antoinette had been a great success and the grandest event ever held in Europe. No one imagined it would be the last wedding of a Dauphin and Dauphine of France.

A VIEW OF VERSAILLES FROM THE LARGE AVENUE BETWEEN THE TWO STABLES BY JEAN BAPTISTE RIGAUD.

UPON HER MARRIAGE, MARIE ANTOINETTE WAS THRUST INTO A GLITTERING, ARTIFICIAL WORLD THAT REVOLVED AROUND THE KING AND OPERATED ON AN UNWRITTEN, HIGHLY DETAILED system of etiquette, the most complex in Europe. She found life inside the château of Versailles, primary official residence of Louis XV, very different from the informal simplicity of Maria Theresa's court in Vienna where she was raised.

The château was filled with the most exquisite paintings, statues, vases and *objets d'art* imaginable. Magnificent Aubusson carpets decorated the floors, and Europe's most renowned furniture makers, including Jean-Henry Reisener (1734–1806) and André-Charles Boulle, supplied cabinets inlaid with brightly coloured exotic woods and unusual desks cleverly designed with concealed compartments and hidden drawers. The food, served on hand-painted Sèvres china, was considered the finest in the country. The gardens, filled with rows of statues and fountains spewing water over eighty feet, were beautiful and lush beyond compare. Marie Antoinette found the grandeur of her new home overwhelming. She felt lost in the labyrinthine palace with its 500 rooms and 1,000 windows. Since Louis XV's wife was dead, the Dauphine was assigned the luxurious suite of rooms used by the queens of France, but the bedchamber was not ready when she arrived. The fabulous ceiling, with panels by François Boucher, had been damaged and was being repainted. Months passed before Marie Antoinette moved into the suite she would occupy for almost two decades. She was temporarily housed in a ground-floor apartment facing the south parterre used by her husband's late father (her first room at Versailles can be seen today and is called the Dauphin's bedchamber).

CHARLES PHILIPPE DE FRANCE, COMTE D'ARTOIS; YOLANDE DE POLASTRON, DUCHESSE DE POLIGNAC (FROM THE PORTRAIT BY ELISABETH-LOUISE VIGÉE-LEBRUN) AND MARIE-THERESE-LOUISE DE SAVOIE-CARIGNAN, PRINCESSE DE LAMBALLE (AFTER EUGENE JOSEPH VIOLLAT).

Marie Antoinette's upbringing had not prepared her for the duties expected of her or the solemnity embraced by the French court. Born in 1755, her childhood was happy and filled with music. She loved playing the harp, could sight-read well, even as a child, and had excellent instructors including composer Christoph Gluck, who served as her singing-master. Maria Theresa's flock of children often performed at family celebrations and attended public and private recitals. In 1762 six-year-old Wolfgang Amadeus Mozart was brought by his father to Vienna to play the harpsichord for the imperial family. Tradition has it that the young prodigy tripped on the polished palace floor after his performance, and Marie Antoinette, who was his age, hurried to help him up. He gratefully thanked her and added that he hoped to marry her some day. The little archduchess responded with a kiss.

Marie Antoinette's education consisted of lessons in deportment, dancing and embroidery. She played with her younger brother and sisters and usually only saw her powerful mother weekly. Governesses raised all of Maria Theresa's daughters and, as the smallest and most amiable, Marie Antoinette could twist her teachers round her finger to the point that they wrote out her letters in pencil for her to trace over in pen. She was still illiterate by the age of 12. When an older sister died of smallpox in 1762, Marie Antoinette suddenly became a pawn in her mother's political machinations. To cement a peace treaty between Austria and France, Maria Theresa quickly prepared her youngest daughter for marriage to Louis XV's heir.

Once in France, the affectionate girl yearned for the companionship and intimacy she had shared with her sisters. Despite the attention lavished on her, she initially had no real friends and, at her mother's suggestion, spent time with the king's daughters Adélaide, Victoire and Sophie: three eccentric, haughty spinsters in their late thirties collectively titled *Mesdames*. British memoirist Horace Walpole, who saw the king's daughters on a visit to Versailles, described them as, "clumsy, plump old wenches, with a bad resemblance to their father ... wearing black cloaks and carrying knitting-bags, not knowing what to say, and wriggling as if they wanted to make water." These unpleasant princesses were Marie Antoinette's main companions during her first 18 months in France.

Surrounded by liveried servants and sycophantic, ruthlessly competitive courtiers, the inexperienced girl suddenly found herself a slave to a never-ending round of daily ceremonies. Almost every moment was planned out for her. In July 1770 she wrote to her mother describing her routine: "I get up at nine… having been dressed, I say my morning prayers, then I breakfast, then go to my aunts [*Mesdames*] where I usually find the king. That goes on until 10.30; at 11.00, I go to have my hair dressed. At 12.00, they call in the chamber, and anyone can come in as long as they belong to the Court. I put on my rouge and wash my hands in front of the whole world; then the men leave and the ladies stay, and I dress in front of them. At noon we have Mass … After Mass we eat in public … From there I go to M. le Dauphin's apartment and, if he is busy, I come back to mine. I read, write or work since I am embroidering a waistcoat for the king which hasn't progressed much, but I hope, with God's grace, it will be finished in a few years." Before her day ended, the Dauphine's schedule included singing and harpsichord lessons, card games, and supper, followed by a family visit to the king.

Marie Antoinette did not grasp the important role etiquette played at Versailles. In the previous century, Louis XIV, the Sun King who ruled for 72 years, presided over carefully choreographed daily ceremonies at court that gave many nobles duties to fulfil, thereby keeping them closely tied to the monarchy. These rituals continued during Louis XV's reign and included the *lever*, the rising and dressing of the king and queen and, in the evenings, the *coucher*, the undressing and putting to bed of royalty. Marie Antoinette, accustomed to etiquette only being used on special occasions, soon dreaded these rituals and pronounced them inconvenient, meaningless, and, worst of all from her point of view, unbelievably dull.

There were a thousand rules to learn: who received a smile, who received a tilt of the head, who was allowed to sit in her presence, and who stood where. Each ceremony consisted of countless nuances. Marie Antoinette tried to ignore the endless admonitions from the Comtesse de Noailles, whom she soon nicknamed "Madame Etiquette". Jeanne Campan later wrote that it was unfortunate that such a stiff, unpleasant woman taught the Dauphine the court's customs and added, "Madame de Noailles abounded in virtues... but etiquette was to her a sort of precious phenomenon; at the slightest change of the correct order, you would have thought that life would forsake her body." The Comtesse de Noailles' approach to educating her mistress did not make the girl compliant; instead, Marie Antoinette balked at this barrage of advice and unwisely began mocking the court's customs. After being thrown from her donkey while riding one day, she lay on the grass laughing and said, "Don't get me up, leave me on the ground. We must wait for Madame Etiquette to show us the exact, correct way to pick up a Dauphine who has fallen off a donkey."

Her pleasures were simple and child-like. Marie Antoinette adored flowers and asked that her rooms be kept filled with roses and tulips. In addition to Mops, her miniature boxer from Vienna, she found other little dogs to pamper and pet. When she had free time, she invited the children of her ladies-in-waiting to play with her until, out of breath and dishevelled, she threw herself into a chair, exhausted from delight at their antics. The Austrian ambassador to France, Comte de Mercy-Argenteau, wrote to her mother in despair, "Madame la Dauphine's first lady-in-waiting has a boy of six or seven and a girl of twelve... The Archduchess spends a large part of her day with these children who spoil and tear her clothes, break the furniture, and cause the greatest disorder in her apartments." Marie Antoinette's unsophisticated, juvenile pleasures proved a sharp contrast to the highly cultured decadence of the king's retinue.

During the eighteenth century, Versailles was a hotbed of malicious gossip and intrigue. The courtiers, rapacious and easily bored, jealously guarded their prerogatives and continually discussed even the most trivial details about the royal family. Marie Antoinette's position as Dauphine made her the subject of constant conjecture; everyone waited for the young foreign girl to make the inevitable gaffe. She was no match for *Mesdames* and other clever ladies who looked on gleefully as the newcomer was easily manipulated to participate in their schemes.

The king's daughters loathed their father's glamorous *maîtresse-en-titre* Jeanne du Barry, a lovely blonde with a disreputable past whom the king ensconced in an apartment that connected to his own by a private staircase. Shortly after Marie Antoinette arrived at Versailles, *Mesdames* began to encourage her to ignore Madame du Barry. They told the virginal girl that she, an Archduchess of Austria and wife of the heir to the throne, should feel incensed that the king expected her to associate with a courtesan. Soon Marie Antoinette refused to speak to Louis XV's mistress. In July 1770, she wrote to her mother that it was "pitiful to see the king's partiality for Madame du Barry, the stupidest, most impertinent creature imaginable." The ill-advised Dauphine compounded her blunder by allowing her ladies to slight the king's favourite. Madame du Barry wept and complained to Louis XV. Infuriated, the king summoned Mercy-Argenteau asking him to change the Dauphine's behaviour. The Austrian ambassador quickly wrote to Marie Theresa, who fired off blistering letters commanding her daughter to make amends to Madame du Barry. The empress reminded the girl that nothing must interfere with the success of the Franco-Austrian alliance. The 16-year-old rebelled and, to the court's amusement, rejected her mother's advice. For 18 months, while the outraged empress attacked Marie Antoinette with lectures, the obstinate teenager unremorsefully snubbed Madame du Barry. The court was in an uproar; some even took bets as to whether the Dauphine would ever capitulate. Finally, after a vitriolic ultimatum from her mother, Marie Antoinette levelled her intense blue eyes at Madame du Barry during a formal reception on New Year's Day 1772, paused, and loudly commented, "There are quite a lot of people here at Versailles today." The remark was brief, but Madame du Barry smiled triumphantly. The king was delighted and embraced the Dauphine. Afterwards

Marie Antoinette bitterly confided to Mercy-Argenteau, "I have spoken to her once, but that is as far as I shall go. Never again shall that woman hear the sound of my voice." This was the first example of how Marie Antoinette's wilfulness verging on implacability, combined with a lack of worldly wisdom, would make her countless enemies.

Even before the Dauphine antagonized the king and his mistress, Maria Theresa did not trust her daughter to strengthen the Franco-Austrian alliance without constant prodding and supervision. She knew Marie Antoinette, bored by politics, disliked intellectual discussion. Although the Dauphine would do anything to please her domineering mother, she was intimidated by the empress and confessed, "I love [her] but I am frightened of her." Marie Antoinette never suspected that, although her mother continually claimed to only care about her daughter's happiness, the empress surrounded her with spies. Many were friends or servants that Marie Antoinette trusted, including Mercy-Argenteau, who considered chicanery an integral part of diplomacy. He unscrupulously forwarded the Dauphine's secrets to the empress in confidential reports. In November 1770, he bragged to Maria Theresa, "I have bought three persons in *Madame l'Archiduchesse's* service… who give me an exact account of all that happens in her private apartments. I am informed day by day of the archduchess's conversations with the Abbé de Vermond [her tutor], and she conceals nothing from him … I have more people and better means still to find out what happens when the king and the Dauphine are together … There is really not an hour of the day when I am not told about what the archduchess has said or done or heard." Although Marie Antoinette never learned who was revealing her behaviour to her mother, she sensed she was being spied upon. This only increased her insecurity, and she soon viewed privacy as the ultimate luxury.

Every day the Dauphine continued trying to win the affection of her husband. Jeanne Campan remembered, "The most mortifying indifference, which frequently degenerated into rudeness, were the sole feelings which the young

PANORAMA OF THE CHÂTEAU DE VERSAILLES.

Collection of the author.

prince then showed toward her … He threw himself, as a matter of duty, upon the bed of the dauphine, and often fell asleep without saying a single word to her." The bride and groom were very different in character. Intensely shy, the Dauphin preferred reading quietly, while his wife loved gaiety and disliked books. Louis-Auguste's interest in fashion was nonexistent; Marie Antoinette delighted in pretty clothes. Discussing history and studying maps were other pleasures his wife did not share, as were the Dauphin's interest in tinkering with locks and collecting unusual clocks and coins. Louis-Auguste enjoyed manual labour and would occasionally pull off his jacket to toil alongside bricklayers or other workers at Versailles. His greatest pleasure was hunting, one of the few things he had in common with his grandfather the king, and often returned to Versailles exhausted after hours in the saddle. Although Louis-Auguste had good qualities – religious devotion, kindness, and sincere humility – these characteristics were not esteemed in the frivolous world of Versailles; the court regarded him as hopeless. Marie Antoinette was soon blamed for her childless marriage, and rumours spread that the Dauphine's lack of fecundity would cause her to be sent back to Austria with her marriage annulled. Maria Theresa, obsessed with the success of Austria's alliance with France, realized her daughter was in a dangerous position and escalated her reproaches to Marie Antoinette for failing to arouse her husband. The Dauphine replied she was still hopeful that Louis-Auguste would soon "make her his wife." But her mother's intimidating letters and the Dauphin's inability to consummate the marriage took its toll on the once-merry girl; her ladies noticed she seemed deeply unhappy and often pensive. When the wife of the Dauphin's cousin had a stillborn child, Marie Antoinette wrote sombrely to her mother that she herself would be glad to have produced even a dead child; at least then no one could say she was not trying to provide France with an heir.

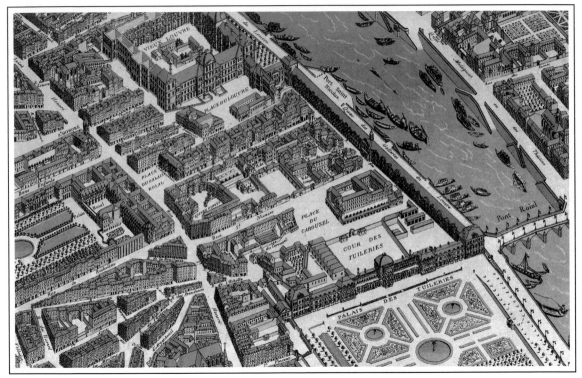

PARIS IN THE 1700S.

MARIE ANTOINETTE'S FIRST DAY IN PARIS

UPON MARIE ANTOINETTE'S ARRIVAL IN FRANCE, SHE EAGERLY ASKED TO TOUR PARIS. INTRIGUED BY STORIES OF THE CITY'S EXTRAORDINARY LANDMARKS – THE LOUVRE AND TUILERIES PALACES, Notre-Dame Cathedral, the Théâtre Français, the Opera and the new church of Sainte-Geneviève – she announced her hope to see as much of the capital as possible.

Over three years later, the exasperated Dauphine had still not spent a single hour in Paris. Well aware that Versailles was only 11 miles from the capital, she repeatedly begged officials to arrange a trip. Her staff scheduled excursions to Paris only to have them cancelled due to behind-the-scenes wrangling; no one could decide who, among the powerful ranks of elite courtiers, had the right to accompany Marie Antoinette when she travelled.

Forbidden to leave Versailles without consent from the monarch, she hesitated to ask Louis XV directly for permission. Traditionally female members of the royal family rarely left court, and the king himself visited the capital infrequently. Blamed by his subjects for losing wars, high taxes and mismanaging state finances, the Parisians loathed Louis XV, who withdrew to the cocoon of his palaces.

Bored with the court's cloistered life at Versailles and unhappily married, Marie Antoinette yearned for diversion from her impotent, eccentric husband, whose latest hobby was climbing to the château's flat roof in the mornings to shoot cats. Although Louis-Auguste gradually warmed to Antoinette, as he called her, and still attempted to consummate their marriage, his efforts remained unsuccessful. No longer a bride but still a virgin, the Dauphine seemed destined to remain childless.

Consumed with maternal longing, she adopted an orphan named Armand whom she first glimpsed while driving through the countryside. Marie Antoinette instructed that the toddler be educated and raised at court. Soon Armand, dressed in lace-edged white suits and tiny shoes with colourful medallions, learned to sing his benefactress's favourite songs. Marie Antoinette encouraged him to play in her rooms and gave the lively child a yapping white puppy. Although Armand provided a welcome distraction, the Dauphine grew gloomy when she contemplated her future. Her ladies-in-waiting felt certain a trip to France's most cosmopolitan city, with its grand buildings, fashionable boutiques and lively atmosphere would lift her spirits. Marie Antoinette heartily concurred.

For once, the adolescent's desires coincided with those of her mother. The Dauphine smiled as she read letter after letter from the empress encouraging her to make an appearance in Paris. Maria Theresa, an experienced diplomat, hoped to strengthen Austria's ties to France. She knew her attractive daughter, though politically inept, could easily endear herself to the style-conscious Parisians.

After much hesitation, Marie Antoinette decided to personally tell the king of her desire to visit the capital. To her surprise, Louis XV seemed pleased and announced that she and her husband should make a grand state visit. He even let the delighted 17-year-old select the day. This walk follows the route taken by Marie Antoinette and Louis-Auguste on their first official trip to Paris on Tuesday 8 June 1773.

On a sunny summer morning, crowds gathered at Versailles and peered through the ornate palace fence at the cortège assembled for the Dauphin and Dauphine's journey. A dozen of Marie Antoinette's ladies laughingly struggled to squeeze their elegant gowns into three carriages. Dignitaries in gilded coaches waited patiently for the young couple to emerge from the palace. When the petite Dauphine and her stocky husband finally appeared, they crossed the Marble Courtyard, which faced east toward Paris, and took their seats in the gleaming royal coach. Pulled by eight magnificent horses with white plumes and a crimson hand-tooled leather harness, the fabulously ornate coach towered over the other vehicles. Footmen and an imposing coachman, all in gorgeous uniforms heavy with golden braid, climbed into position. To the cracking of whips, the procession set off down Avenue de Paris, then, as now, the middle of three tree-lined *allées* radiating outward from the front of the château.

Enthusiastic crowds, two and three deep, lined the entire route from Versailles to Paris. At the western edge of the city, a military escort, led by the king's personal bodyguard, joined the cortège. Blue-coated French Guards and red-coated Swiss troops surrounded the royal coach, while 24 foot soldiers marched alongside.

Just after 11.00 am, cannon placed around the city announced the Dauphin and Dauphine's arrival. As a light breeze rippled the Seine, a contingent of dignitaries gathered nearby at the Cours la Reine, one of the city's main entrances. When the caravan of coaches topped the hill of Chaillot, the town orchestra stuck up a lively air. Waiting at the edge of the river was the Governor of Paris, elderly Maréchal de Brissac, in a gold-lace suit with jewelled orders blazing on his chest. Brissac enthusiastically greeted the heirs to the throne and, as lackeys held open the door of the royal coach, Louis-Auguste and Marie Antoinette descended to accept the traditional welcoming gift: golden keys to the city gates presented on a shining silver tray.

A large group of market women, dressed in their best clothes, stepped forward. Local custom allowed the *poissardes* (fishwives) and other female vendors to address the royal family on important occasions. The eldest delivered a brief speech to Marie Antoinette saluting her as their future queen. After she finished, the others presented the girl with their finest wares: fragrant red roses and ripe, large oranges. Then the *femmes des Halles*, named for Paris' ancient food market, laughingly began to shout crude sexual advice to the couple. The Dauphin and Dauphine, who knew

PARIS IN THE 1770S

Although Paris looked very different in the 1700s, many landmarks and streets from that era still exist. Eighteenth-century Paris was a walled metropolis of splendour and squalor, and many of the city's quartiers dated to medieval times. The capital, consisting of about 8,000 acres, housed over half a million inhabitants whose lives coexisted in the starkest contrast. The country's richest lived there, as did the poorest; illiterate beggars and the most cultivated intellectuals in France. Rousseau only slightly exaggerated when he claimed that Paris, of all Europe's cities, was the one, "where fortunes are most unequal, and where flaunted wealth and the most appalling poverty dwell together."

Paris then had over a thousand streets, most of them crammed with pedestrians. Coaches and sedan chairs created constant traffic jams, along with livestock herded through the city. Vendors hawked their wares and shouted, "Brandy", "Cold Water", "Fine Oysters" and "Fresh Cherries, just picked!". The tumult of the main thoroughfares such as the Rue Saint-Honoré on the Right Bank was deafening. Sewage ran down an open trench in the middle of larger streets; foul smells were overpowering.

Considered the cultural centre of Europe, Paris hummed with artists and artisans, writers and intellectuals, restaurants (the first appeared in Paris in the 1760s) and fine shops far surpassing those in London and other European cities. Although only the Comédie-Française could perform plays in French until the 1780s, the capital had many theatres. A fascination with couture, hairdressing and make-up ruled the upper and middle class Parisian women.

rumours of their unconsummated marriage had spread, blushed and managed to smile. Embarrassed titters rose from the crowd as the high-spirited market women escalated their bawdy suggestions and even made obscene hand gestures. Several remarks implied the fault lay with Marie Antoinette, who was visibly relieved when she could escape this ordeal by climbing back into the royal coach.

Follow the Quai des Tuileries along the Seine, cross the Pont Royal at the Louvre, turn left and proceed along the river using the Quai Voltaire, which becomes Quai Malaquais. When you pass the French Institute on your right, the Quai Malaquais becomes the Quai de Conti.

THE ROYAL MINT, OR HÔTEL DES MONNAIES, AND INSTITUT DE FRANCE ON THE BANKS OF THE SEINE.

Collection of the author.

STOP ONE: HÔTEL DES MONNAIES

11, QUAI DE CONTI

Métro: Pont-Neuf, Saint-Germain-des-Prés

SOON THE PROCESSION FOLLOWED THE CURVES OF THE MURKY SEINE INTO THE HEART OF THE CITY. AS LOUIS-AUGUSTE AND MARIE ANTOINETTE SLOWLY DROVE THROUGH TRIUMPHAL ARCHES erected in their honour, the people of Paris greeted them with wild applause and tossed flowers into the streets. Houses and shops along the route were decorated with brilliant tapestries and bright carnations and tuberoses. The cortège snaked along the riverfront until the Quai de Conti, where the carriages stopped at the Royal Mint: the first of two new buildings the couple would inspect that day designed in a style reflecting a return to antiquity later known as neoclassicism. Although still under construction when Louis-Auguste and Marie Antoinette visited, the Mint looks very much the same today as in the 1770s.

In the front courtyard, the Dauphin and Dauphine met the building's prefect, who described the coining process and pointed out the squadrons that guarded the currency. Marie Antoinette, bestowing smiles on everyone, did not know that the Royal Mint served as a symbol of France's financial disorder. As the aristocracy and clergy paid a much lower percentage of their income in taxes than others, the burden of financing the government fell heavily on the country's poor and middle class: the workers and merchants.

Though France stayed in debt, the king continued to spend recklessly. His stables housed several thousand horses with 200 coaches and carriages waiting to carry him from palace to palace, just as centuries of Bourbon kings had done. Some 295 cooks prepared food for Louis XV, and 150 pages served it. Besides his official mistress, the

MARIE ANTOINETTE ON A STATE VISIT TO PARIS,
A DRAWING BY J. M. MOREAU.

monarch kept a brothel in Versailles, a little house near the palace in the Parc au Cerfs. For decades Louis XV bedded barely pubescent girls in this private harem, estimated to cost the French over a half million dollars annually.

Once called "Louis le Bien-Aimé" (Louis the Well Beloved), the king's unpopularity soared during the early 1770s. Although aware of the high cost of his pleasures, Louis XV refused to economize and wryly predicted, "Après moi le déluge" (After me, the deluge). When cautioned by ministers that the country faced bankruptcy, the king shrugged and replied, "Things as they are will last through my time." Louis XV bequeathed this financial legacy to his grandson and Marie Antoinette, who were never able to escape impending financial ruin. When the young couple ascended the throne, their enemies accused them of wasting France's wealth on luxuries, but their expenditures did not cause the country's financial predicament. The monarchy went bankrupt because of military expenses and poor management.

Walk down Quai de Conti. Turn left and cross the Pont-Neuf. Turn right and walk down Quai des Orfèvres, which will become Quai du Marché Neuf, which leads to Notre-Dame.

NOTRE-DAME DE PARIS FROM AN ETCHING BY NICHOLAS PERELLE.

STOP TWO: NOTRE-DAME DE PARIS

6, PLACE DU PARVIS-NOTRE-DAME

Métro: Cité

L EAVING THE MINT, THE CORTÈGE CROSSED THE SEINE ON PARIS'S OLDEST AND MOST HEAVILY TRAVELLED BRIDGE, THE PONT-NEUF. THICK CROWDS CAUSED THE PROCESSION TO SLOW TO a crawl. Trumpets rang out as the Dauphin and Dauphine watched a grand military display staged across from the bronze equestrian statue of Henri IV on the bridge.

Bells rang in the belfry of Notre-Dame as the cortège neared the great Gothic cathedral, which was more splendid than it is today (gold was removed during the Revolution). The Archbishop of Paris greeted the royal couple in the nearby square, then lined with old houses set on narrow streets. The couple stepped from the bright glare of the early afternoon sun into the dim light of the cathedral, then stopped for a moment until their eyes became accustomed to the shadowy darkness. They followed the Archbishop across the church behind the raised high altar to the elegant Chapel of the Virgin, where the king's *chapelain*, assisted by the clergy, presided over a special Mass.

Louis-Auguste, more devout than his wife, followed the service intently while onlookers noticed that Marie Antoinette stifled a yawn. The ceremony ended with a large choir singing a solemn motif in beautiful harmony.

Walk across the Place du Parvis-Notre-Dame in front of the cathedral. Turn left onto Rue de la Cité. Cross the Seine on the Petit Pont. Walk south on Rue du Petit-Point, which becomes Rue Saint-Jacques. Pass Boulevard Saint-Germain and Rue des Ecoles. Turn left onto Rue Cujas, and continue until you see the columns of the Panthéon.

THE PANTHÉON.

Collection of the author.

STOP THREE: SAINTE-GENEVIÈVE (PANTHÉON)

PLACE DU PANTHÉON

Métro: Luxembourg

L EAVING NOTRE-DAME, THE GILDED COACHES VEERED SOUTH INTO THE LATIN QUARTER, NAMED FOR THE LANGUAGE SPOKEN AT THE UNIVERSITY OF PARIS IN THE MIDDLE AGES. AFTER STOPPING at the college of Louis-le-Grand, the carriages climbed to the top of Montagne Sainte-Geneviève, the steepest hill in Paris, to visit a new church. Like the Hôtel des Monnaies, the Panthéon, then the church of Sainte-Geneviève, was still under construction during Marie Antoinette and Louis-Auguste's visit. Although uncompleted, it was one of the latest sights for travellers to visit and already considered one of the most beautiful churches in France. The Dauphin and Dauphine admired the building's windows, which have since been enclosed, and massive front doors. A masterpiece of architecture and early French classicism, the church's great dome still towers over the Left Bank.

Leaving the Pantheon, turn right and walk across the Place du Panthéon. Continue straight on Rue Clovis. The church of Saint-Etienne-du-Mont will be on your left. Turn left on Rue du Cardinal-Lemoine and proceed to the Metro (Cardinal-Lemoine stop). Take the No. 10 Métro (toward Boulogne-Pont de Saint-Cloud) five stops to the Sevres-Babylone station. Transfer there to the No 12 Métro (towards Porte de la Chapelle) to the Concorde stop. The Jardin des Tuileries is the big garden east of Place de la Concorde. The Tuileries palace sat between the arch (Arc de Triomphe du Carrousel) and the garden.

THE ELEGANT AND FORMAL TUILERIES GARDENS FROM AN ETCHING BY NICOLAS DE POILLY.

STOP FOUR: JARDIN DES TUILERIES

PLACE DE LA CONCORDE

Métro: Tuileries, Concorde

THE YOUNG COUPLE ARRIVED FOR A LATE AFTERNOON DINNER AT THE CHÂTEAU DES TUILERIES, AN ENORMOUS THREE-STOREY PALACE THAT STRETCHED BETWEEN THE Louvre and Place Louis XV, now Place de la Concorde. The Tuileries, named after the tile factories that dominated this area of Paris when Catherine de Médicis commissioned the building of a palace in the 1500s, was burned in 1871; the ruins were torn down in 1882. The formal gardens that sat behind the palace still exist and are open to the public.

During the 1700s, the Tuileries gardens were usually opened to the public only once a year on the holiday of the Feast Day of Saint-Louis, although well-to-do families were allowed to stroll through the lush, ornate gardens on Sundays. Now all well-dressed Parisians were invited to enter the palace on the day of the Dauphin and Dauphine's state visit. After climbing the grand staircase, with footmen clad in scarlet standing on every other stair, spectators stood on a balcony that overlooked the grand banquet set out for the couple. A constant flow of visitors watched Marie Antoinette and Louis-Auguste enjoying their elaborate meal. Twenty-seven ladies in formal court gowns dined with the Dauphine and her ladies, while only men ate at the Dauphin's table. Golden fleurs-de-lis, the emblem of the Bourbons, decorated the walls and carpets of the salon. Frescos, fountains, and thousands of rare flowers in costly vases filled the hall. High above the multicoloured marble floor, massive crystal chandeliers flickered with hundreds of candles. Statues of bronze goddesses holding massive candelabra, commissioned by the king at the time of Louis-

PHILIBERT-LOUIS DEBUCOURT'S PAINTING OF A ROWDY CARNIVAL IN THE VICINITY OF LES HALLES IN PARIS.

akg-images

Auguste's wedding to Marie Antoinette, decorated the salon and ensured that the room glowed with light. Endless trays brought delicacies, prepared by Paris's best chefs, to the tables, sparkling with gold and silver plate.

At the crown's expense, a lavish dinner had also been prepared for the market women in the palace's concert-hall. The light-hearted *femmes des Halles* eagerly launched into their meal of various roasts and gigantic pyramids of fruit and dessert. Undaunted by the splendour of the palace, the women laughed and sang as they feasted on delicacies such as asparagus, strawberry tarts and sorbet. Their raucous voices and lively banter echoed down the palace's marble hallways and provided a whimsical contrast to the hushed solemnity of the Dauphin and Dauphine's meal.

After dinner, invited guests gathered to meet the young couple in one of the Tuileries' luxurious reception rooms. Louis-Auguste and Marie Antoinette stepped onto the balcony overlooking the gardens, packed with well-wishers. Bright afternoon sun washed over the heir to the throne and his wife as thousands shouted "*Vive Madame la Dauphine! Vive Monseigneur le Dauphin!*" The young couple happily appeared on the balcony ten times to accept the acclaim; they both made a point of waving to acknowledge the crowd, novel for royalty in the 1700s. Marie Antoinette received more cheers than her husband, and the timid Dauphin stepped to one side, glad to let her have the spotlight.

Dressed in an exquisite low-cut crème-coloured silk gown, Marie Antoinette smiled coquettishly at the multitude of happy faces. As the adulation washed over her, she raised one tiny embroidered glove to her mouth, paused, and blew a kiss. The enraptured crowd cheered, threw hats in the air, and waved handkerchiefs. Marie Antoinette's huge blue eyes gazed down into the sea of faces. Eager to please, she instinctively sank into a deep curtsey. The Parisians answered with roars of delight as she held the pose for several minutes, her mountain of snow-white powdered hair tilted precariously forward. When she finally arose, the Governor of Paris shouted over the din, "Madame, you now have 200,000 lovers."

Thrilled, Marie Antoinette grabbed her reluctant husband by the hand and pulled him into the gardens. She insisted on walking with the strollers gathered on the sloping terrace along the Seine, then, as now, called the Terrasse du Bord de l'Eau. Surrounded by well-wishers, the young couple was quickly hemmed in and unable to move. Both the Dauphin and Dauphine repeatedly told bodyguards not to hurt anyone while pushing their way through the throng. The heirs to the throne finally arrived at the terrace overlooking Place Louis XV (now Place de la Concorde). They stayed for 30 minutes amidst joyful pandemonium before returning to Versailles.

For the first time since she arrived in France, Marie Antoinette felt loved and accepted. Elated, she described the scene to her mother, "We were received with all imaginable honour. Though this was pleasant, what touched me much more was the affection and zeal of the poor people, which, though crushed by taxation, was overflowing with joy at the sight of us. On our way home from the palace, we walked for half an hour upon an open terrace. The crowd was so great that we were blocked for three quarters of an hour without being able to move forward or backward... How lucky we are, considering our rank and position, to have gained the affection of the people so easily."

The Parisians now adored Marie Antoinette, and her popularity was never higher than as Dauphine. The city euphorically praised the glamorous queen-to-be, who fell in love with Paris, and burning with anticipation, returned again and again to the capital. Often she travelled in state by day, attended by the court, to watch public festivities. Sometimes, accompanied only by family members, she visited the Théâtre Français. Occasionally, as when she went to the opera to hear Sophie Arnould, France's most popular singer, the Dauphin joined her. She toured the Bibliothèque du Roi [see Other Places, page 151] and the Salon, a prestigious art exhibition of new works, at the Louvre. She attended fairs, shopped at boutiques, and watched open-air dancing exhibitions. Captivated by the city, she began to travel to Paris two or three times a week. Soon Marie Antoinette danced all night at masked balls where she could mingle with strangers and, in her naïveté, believe no one recognized her. Then she and her ladies rushed back to Versailles, scandalizing the court by arriving at seven in the morning and attending Mass before falling into bed.

Three or four years of visiting the cosmopolitan city transformed the gauche Austrian girl into an elegant woman, a fashion trendsetter whose taste was shaped by the decadence of the most stylish city in Europe. Marie Antoinette became obsessed with her appearance and began to spend hours with the best milliners, dressmakers, hairdressers and jewellers. Soon she devoted herself to the pursuit of pleasure with an astonishing single-mindedness. Paris offered everything she adored: dancing, music, entertainment and adventure. The joyous acclaim she received there – and the freedom she enjoyed – only increased her disdain for Versailles' strict etiquette. She became determined to rid herself of these rules as soon as possible. In her naïveté, she believed the French loved her and would love her forever.

VIEW OF THE TRIANON BY THE CHEVALIER DE LESPINASSES.

Collection of the author.

THE PETIT TRIANON

"You like flowers, well, I have a whole bouquet to give you: the Petit Trianon."
Louis XVI to Marie Antoinette in 1774, the first year of his reign

IN THE SPRING OF 1774, LOUIS XV CONTRACTED SMALLPOX WHILE STAYING WITH MADAME DU BARRY AT THE PETIT TRIANON, A THREE-STOREY SQUARE NEOCLASSICAL MANSION TUCKED INTO A CORNER of the park at Versailles. On 10 May, the 64-year-old monarch died. When told they had become king and queen, Louis-Auguste and Marie Antoinette, sitting together in the Dauphine's rooms, fell to their knees, overwhelmed, and prayed, "Protect us, dear God. We are too young to reign."

The 19-year-old Louis-Auguste now became Louis XVI, absolute monarch of France. The new king announced, "I should like to be loved [by my people]", and the country hoped for great reforms from this unassuming young ruler. Despite his good intentions, the erratically educated Louis XVI was ill-prepared to reign. He had no experience dealing with ministers and reached decisions with such difficulty that his brother, the Comte de Provence, joked that trying to get an answer from the king resembled "attempting to hold oiled billiard balls together."

Traditionally, French kings took mistresses and the court eagerly waited to see if this custom would be perpetuated; but Louis XVI had fallen deeply in love with Marie Antoinette, and no other woman interested him. Dazzled by his attractive wife but still unable to consummate their marriage, he tried to please her by paying her debts and rarely denying her requests. She longed for a country home with a private garden, and one of Louis's first acts as king was to give her the Petit Trianon, originally called the Palais de Flore. He presented his wife with the master key, glittering with diamonds, and said, ""You like flowers, well, I have a whole bouquet to give you: the Petit Trianon. This lovely spot has always been the residence of the king's favourite: therefore it must be yours." For the next 15 years, this small Grecian-style château would be Marie Antoinette's private home.

She quickly relayed the news to her mother and, on 16 June, the empress replied, "The generosity of the king regarding Trianon, said to be the most agreeable of houses, gives me great pleasure …" but soon warned, "Do not draw the king into unnecessary expenditures; let not this first present lead to great expenses, and even less to extravagance … I fear only your laziness and dissipation." Determined to personalize this new residence, the queen dressed her footmen in her own colours, scarlet with silver embroidery, and asked that her initials replace the late king's cipher interwoven in the ornate iron banister of the main staircase. At the gates of the Trianon park, she had rules posted, which she signed, bearing the heading "By Order of the Queen," instead of the traditional "By Order of the King." Disgusted with Versailles' dirty passageways and filthy courtyards filled with slop water thrown from upper windows, Marie Antoinette ordered that her home be kept as a model of cleanliness.

Because the Petit Trianon had been built in Louis's XV's private botanical garden, various shades of green decorated the house, and the décor revolved around motifs of horticulture. Panels of gilded roses, sunflowers, and lilies decorated the salons, which were warmed by fireplaces sculpted with apples and grapes. Designed by Louis XV's favourite architect Jacques-Ange Gabriel, the Trianon was built on uneven ground. Gabriel cleverly concealed this by making two sides of the house appear to have different ground floors. The front courtyard led into the lowest floor, which held two guardrooms, the imposing main staircase, and, eventually, a billiards room. The first floor was filled with larger salons: the dining rooms and reception room. The queen transformed one corner of this floor, previously part of a staircase, into a boudoir. Her bedroom, with a small bed originally used by Madame du Barry, had two large windows facing north overlooking the garden, and she filled this simple room with souvenirs of her childhood: an Austrian map, a painting of Vienna, and images of her brothers and sisters. Marie Antoinette and her mother collected Japanese lacquer objects, which they sent to each other as gifts. The queen kept part of her large collection here: cleverly designed boxes shaped like fans, roosters and little dogs. A small staircase on one side of the house led to the attic, which held a cluster of small rooms used by the queen's closest friends and the king's younger sister, Madame Elisabeth. Louis XVI had his own attic apartment, but rarely used it and never spent the night.

Although her new possession was only a ten-minute carriage ride from the main château, the queen preferred to travel on foot. Madame Campan described her as, "dressed in white, with a plain straw hat … followed by a single servant through the walks leading to the Petit Trianon." Preoccupied with remodelling the house and garden, the queen cancelled many official appointments, and ambassadors would sometimes drive from Paris in bad weather for an audience only to find that she had not returned from Trianon.

Marie Antoinette believed royalty should be allowed privacy, and loathed Versailles. She concentrated on making the Trianon an insular world where she could relax. She instructed her guests not to treat her as queen while at Trianon. No ladies were to stand when she entered the room; she wanted them to continue working at their needlepoint or playing billiards. She abandoned court dress for a simple muslin gown tied with a sash and asked her friends to dress casually. Because she hoped to recreate the informality of her mother's court, Petit Trianon was soon nicknamed "Petit Vienne" and gossip spread that the queen had only German spoken at her home.

Although the grounds of Versailles remained open to anyone, no one entered the Trianon area without an invitation from Marie Antoinette, who teased her husband saying that even he could visit only when requested. She personally

MOVING MIRRORS & FLYING TABLES

Always obsessed with privacy, Marie Antoinette ordered that an unusual set of moving mirrors be installed in her boudoir at the Petit Trianon. The resulting room, the cabinet des glaces mouvantes, *has become one of the most famous in the world. Large mirrors, in golden frames, descended into recessed pockets by day so the queen could enjoy her view of the park. In the evenings, these mirrors, controlled by an intricate system of pulleys, covered the windows so no curious eyes could spy on her. This inventive mechanism, still installed at the Trianon, caused gossip that the queen held orgies in this small salon, although her pleasures were simple child-like games like blind-man's buff or eating strawberries and cream on a garden bench. Mique designed the queen's boudoir, decorated with pale blue and white woodwork delicately laden with garlands, cornucopias, and lyres, and her cipher remains carved in the intricate panelling.*

A generation earlier, Louis XV, also seeking privacy, commissioned a "flying table" for the Petit Trianon's dining room. Invented by an artist/mechanic named Loriot, this table volante *lowered to a ground-floor kitchen, then filled with trays of food, and raised back to the dining room. While servants prepared the platters, a metal flower covered the spot where the table had been. This elaborate dumbwaiter, displayed at the Louvre in 1769 before its installation, eliminated the need for servants at Louis XV's intimate suppers. The king used a similar table at Choisy-le-Roi, another royal home, and commissioned a large central table and four smaller ones called* postillions *(servants) for the Petit Trianon. Although they no longer exist, the floor of the large dining salon still bears the marks of the mechanism.*

reviewed letters asking to tour her park and decided who would receive one of the *jetons*, or tokens that allowed entry. Entrance to the château was restricted to the queen's small circle of friends, and porters locked the gates to the rest of the court. This excluded most of the old nobility, and the 20-year-old queen showed indifference to their complaints. She ignored the advice of older staff members, who urged her to placate these powerful courtiers, spend less time at the Trianon, and devote herself to her duties. Instead, Marie Antoinette visited her new home as often as possible, playing cards, walking in the garden and entertaining her guests by serving dainty meals. She filled the Trianon with furnishings that reflected her personal taste and commissioned exquisite pieces including a set of chairs by Georges Jacob.

The Petit Trianon was so small that few of the queen's entourage could stay there. Usually the first close friend she made, Marie-Thérèse of Savoy, the Princesse de Lamballe, attended her. A beautiful, devout young widow with flowing blonde hair, the Princesse de Lamballe was six years older than Marie Antoinette and had been married to a relative of the royal family. Extremely sensitive, the Princesse de Lamballe cried easily, fainted at the sight of shrimp and other crustaceans, and once swooned after seeing a lobster in a painting. Marie Antoinette gave her the prestigious position of Superintendent of the Household, but quickly grew bored with her overemotional friend.

In August 1775, the queen heard a sweet-faced young woman, 26-year-old Yolande de Polignac, wife of Comte Jules de Polignac, singing at a court fête and asked to meet her. From a noble but impecunious family rarely seen at court, this lively blue-eyed brunette, amused the queen, who soon spent every spare minute with her new friend singing duets and sharing leisurely tête-à-têtes. For almost 14 years, Marie Antoinette showered favours and appointments on the Comtesse de Polignac and her ambitious family, who became adept at manipulating the queen and isolating her from the court. Soon anonymous pamphlets described lurid accounts of life at Trianon labelling Marie Antoinette a lesbian and adulteress. She complained to her mother that these libellous booklets had become "an epidemic …

Both tastes are freely attributed to me: for women and for lovers." She enjoyed the company of her husband's younger brother, the frivolous Comte d'Artois, although their relationship was platonic. He brought unusual amusements to Trianon including a troupe of pantomimes and a famous acrobat named *le Petit Diable*, who performed tricks on the tightrope without a balancing pole. Marie Antoinette complimented this acrobat so much that the Comte d'Artois secretly took lessons until he could perform the same feats for her. This led to gossip that they were lovers.

Maria Theresa, concerned about Marie Antoinette's sullied reputation and the lack of an heir to seal the Franco-Austrian alliance, urged her son, Emperor Joseph II, to travel to Paris and advise his sister. In April 1777, 36-year-old Joseph arrived at Versailles for a six-week visit. Marie Antoinette drove her eldest brother to Trianon for dinner. After the meal, they walked alone in the garden, and the queen confided in Joseph about her passionless relationship with her husband. Several weeks later Joseph met with the king, who told his brother-in-law many intimate details of his marriage. Joseph, stunned at the king's revelations, described Louis's problem to his brother Archduke Leopold, "Imagine, in his marriage bed – here is the secret – he has strong, perfectly good erections; he introduces the member, stays there without moving for about two minutes, withdraws without ejaculating but still erect, and bids her goodnight ... And the king is satisfied with this." Joseph reminded his brother-in-law of the importance of providing France with an heir and instructed the king on the basics of reproduction. Around this time, Louis may have undergone an operation to cure his phymosis, as Marie Antoinette soon wrote joyfully to her mother that the marriage had finally been consummated after seven years. On 19 December 1778, Marie Antoinette gave birth to a daughter named Marie-Thérèse-Charlotte, with the title Madame Royale. As was the custom, the queen gave birth before the entire court in her bedchamber at Versailles. Even the public was allowed to observe and, to the horror of the ladies-in-waiting, several overzealous men climbed on the furniture to get a better view.

Marie Antoinette began planning her garden as soon as she acquired Trianon, but work was delayed for two years as Turgot, France's Controller General, refused to approve the budget to rebuild the park as the queen wished. She hated formal gardens and announced that lines of trees and geometric flowerbeds, as laid out at Versailles by Louis XIV's renowned gardener Le Nôtre, bored her. She had seen several charming *jardins anglo-chinois* near Paris at Parc Monceau and Chantilly [see Other Places, pages 152, 156] and adored their winding walks and *fabriques*, ornamental man-made sights including Grecian ruins, a temple and pyramids. Soon she ordered Louis XV's hothouses demolished and his vast botanical garden moved to the Jardin des Plantes in Paris. Finally, in 1777, her horticulturists and architects, led by Richard Mique, began work on her romantic, informal garden. The queen insisted that models be shown to her and, if not pleased, requested that the work be redone. She urged her staff to hurry, and a letter from the Warden of the King's Storehouse to Mique stated, "you know our mistress, and that she likes to enjoy her pleasures without delay." Artificial mountains, rivers and a lake were quickly built, along with a grotto that held a small waterfall. The Comte d'Hézecques described it as, "so dark that the eyes required time to discover what objects it contained. Carpeted with moss, the grotto was freshened by a stream, and the bed of moss was an invitation to repose. But, whether by chance or by design, a crevice, opening at the top of the moss made it possible to look out over the entire meadow and to see in the distance anyone approaching." A hidden back exit made it possible to leave the grotto discreetly.

Two of the loveliest additions to Trianon can still be seen: the Belvédère and the Temple de l'Amour, commissioned by Marie Antoinette in 1778. Inspired by the Temple of the Sybil in Tivoli, Mique built the classical Temple de l'Amour, a cupola supported by a dozen Corinthian columns, on a man-made island with a stream separating it from the house. He placed it so it could be seen from the royal bedroom. The temple held Bouchardon's statue "Cupid cutting his Bow from Hercules' Club"; the original statue, now in the Louvre, has been replaced with a copy.

PILLARS OF RUBIES, FLOORS OF GOLD

During the 1780s, gossip spread about the escalating sums spent by Marie Antoinette on Trianon. Anonymous pamphlets circulated throughout Paris claimed that France faced bankruptcy because the queen walked on golden floors while precious stones covered the walls of her salons. The rumours may have started when coloured glass was used in a theatrical set during a play performed at Trianon.

In April 1789, the deputies of the States General arrived at Versailles from all parts of France. Eager to sightsee, they asked for a tour of the queen's château. She granted their request, and the men hurried to Trianon anxious to view rooms glittering with diamonds and pillars encrusted with rubies and sapphires. When they saw the simple decorations, they insisted Marie Antoinette had redecorated because of their visit. One of the key accusations at her trial in 1792 was that she had "depleted the national treasury" with unnecessary expenditure at her home. The prosecutor asked where she got the vast amounts of money spent on Trianon "where she always played a goddess" and Marie Antoinette replied, "It is possible that the Petit Trianon cost huge sums of money, perhaps more than I would have wished; for I gradually became involved by degrees. I desire, more than anybody, to be informed of what was actually spent there."

The Belvédère, a stone octagonal building constructed on a small hill, was similar to a nearby pavilion designed in 1750 by Gabriel for Louis XV. Marie Antoinette could not resist the view from its tiny drawing room and liked to rest here in the afternoon. The Belvédère's plain facade concealed a lavish interior with decorated stucco walls, an ornate ceiling depicting cupids hovering in the sky, and a gorgeous mosaic floor in blue, green, white and red marble. Then, as now, eight small smiling sphinxes sat outside watching over the garden.

By the late 1770s, this Anglo-Chinese fairyland was almost finished, and, to Marie Antoinette's delight, the old botanical garden was unrecognizable. The Duc de Croÿ, a gardening enthusiast, was an eyewitness to these alterations: "I went to the Trianon having not been there since Louis XV's death … I thought I must be mad or dreaming when, in place of the great hothouse that was the most precious in all Europe, I saw mountains of a considerable size, a big rock and a stream. Never have two acres of land been so completely changed, nor cost so much money!"

In September 1778, Marie Antoinette hosted her first lavish fête at Trianon. A country fair had been constructed with ladies of the court sitting in little booths acting as vendors. A faux market housed a bakery, candy shop and tavern, where the queen served lemonade to her guests. The band of the French Guards performed while clowns from the Comédie-Française entertained the crowd. Magnificent fêtes were then given for her brother (Joseph II) and for the Russian Tsarevich. In May 1782 the Baroness d'Oberkirch, who travelled to France with the Russian royal family, toured the queen's estate and, delighted, wrote a description: "Early this morning I visited the Petit Trianon of the queen. Goodness, what a delicious walk! Beautiful groves scented with lilac, filled with the charming songs of a thousand nightingales. The weather was magnificent, the air loaded with the balmy odours of spring flowers; butterflies stretched their golden wings, gilded in the rays of the spring sunshine. Never in my life have I spent a more enchanting time than those three hours visiting this retreat. Although the château is not large, it is very well

THE TEMPLE DE L'AMOUR, IN THE GROUNDS OF THE TRIANON, BY THE CHEVALIER DE LEPINASSE.

arranged … with the greatest taste and magnificence … and can easily accommodate a great number of persons. The grounds possess every imaginable decoration … winding paths, grottoes, sheets of water, cascades, mountains, temples, statues; in short everything that could diversify or beautify the view." The Baroness d'Oberkirch sat at a supper in honour of the Russian heir and reported that over 300 guests were served a menu consisting of "eight soups, eight egg-dishes, 48 entrées, 16 roasts, 16 large sweets, and 48 small desserts."

Marie Antoinette held the most lavish reception at the Petit Trianon in July 1784 for Gustavus III, King of Sweden, who wrote a vivid account, "We took supper in the garden pavilions; afterwards the *jardin anglais* was illuminated. It was perfectly enchanting. The queen chose not to sit at table, preferring to look after the needs of her guests like the most attentive of hostesses." The festivities heightened after the sun set and Madame Campan recorded that, "Earthen lamps, concealed by boards painted green, threw light upon the beds of shrubs and flowers, and brought out their varied tints. Several hundred burning fagots in the moat behind the Temple of Love made a blaze of light, which rendered that spot the most brilliant in the garden."

In the 1780s, Marie Antoinette allowed many visitors to see her estate and, in the summer, gave a ball every Sunday in the gardens. She invited children from the nearby village to these balls and asked their governesses to introduce the little boys and girls to her. By then, some of the high nobility, resentful at being snubbed, had stopped coming to Versailles and no longer cared to visit the queen. Although Marie Antoinette never built a palace or mansion like so many French queens and royal mistresses, the huge sums spent on Trianon was a factor in her loss of popularity.

MARIE ANTOINETTE BY JEAN-FRANÇOIS JANINET, 1777.
Collection of the author.

THE QUEEN'S PETITS APPARTEMENTS AT VERSAILLES

Marie Antoinette's private apartments in the main château of Versailles still exist and remain much the same as when she left them in 1789. They can be toured in a small group; a separate tour is available for Louis XVI's private rooms. Each lasts an hour and a half and is usually only conducted in French. As different parts of the château are shown each day, call Versailles in the morning at (33–1) 30 83 77 89 to see which tours are being offered, or arrive when the château opens and proceed to Entrance D for information and tickets. A calendar of events and more information can be found at: www.chateauversailles.fr

"In my personal cabinets… I will enjoy the comforts of private life, which do not exist for royalty unless we have the wit to procure them for ourselves." Marie Antoinette

ON 22 OCTOBER 1781, AFTER MORE THAN 11 YEARS OF MARRIAGE, MARIE ANTOINETTE FINALLY GAVE BIRTH TO A SON, LOUIS-JOSEPH. THRILLED, LOUIS XVI TOLD HER, "MADAME, YOU HAVE FULFILLED our wishes, and those of France." The nation rejoiced at the birth of the heir to the throne, and the queen briefly regained her popularity. Sadly, her mother died one year before the birth of the Dauphin and, with the death of the empress, the young queen lost the only person whose counsel could really have anchored her.

After the Dauphin's birth, Louis gave his 25-year-old wife use of a small octagonal boudoir, the *Méridienne*, where she could rest between audiences in the middle of the day. She commissioned architect Richard Mique, then finishing the Grotto at the Petit Trianon, to transform this salon, behind her official bedchamber, into an opulent sitting room that resembled the inside of a jewel box. Mique kept the ceiling and floor unadorned but covered the

THE QUEEN'S MINISTER OF FASHION

Marie Antoinette never officially named a "Minister of Fashion" but Rose Bertin (1747–1813), the queen's dressmaker for 20 years, wielded tremendous influence and created dozens of styles copied throughout Europe. Although Marie Antoinette employed other great dressmakers, such as Madame Eloffe, who supplied bodices and everyday frocks, Mademoiselle Rose, as Bertin was known, created almost all of the queen's court dresses, including many immortalized in celebrated portraits.

When Marie Antoinette arrived in France, Bertin provided some of her trousseau, but the two did not meet for several years. When finally summoned to Versailles, the perceptive modiste *quickly grasped that Marie Antoinette wanted to dazzle Europe with her style and be the originator of French fashion. Soon Bertin could add the title of "Purveyor to Her Majesty" to the signboard outside her shop in Paris [see page 150], and the dressmaker travelled to Versailles twice a week.*

Although called a milliner (or marchande de modes, *a fashion merchant who trimmed gowns already fitted by a dressmaker), Bertin designed the* tout ensemble: *elegant dresses and shoes to compliment her elaborate headdresses and bonnets. She incorporated romance and fantasy into her creations, and the queen's eyes sparkled as she slipped on shoes with a row of emeralds glittering on the heel, dresses with seductive names like "choked sighs" and "indiscreet tears" and cunning bonnets adorned with fur and the finest lace. The queen refused to wear anything passé, and her thirst for new fashion pressured Bertin to constantly create; in May 1782, a typical month, she invented over 30 new headdresses.*

Marie Antoinette adored Bertin's pouf à la circonstance, *a large showy headdress commemorating topical events. A mourning* pouf *appeared just after the death of Louis XV, quickly followed by the inoculation* pouf *to commemorate the new king and his brothers undergoing vaccination to prevent smallpox. This headdress featured a rising sun and an olive tree bearing a serpent, the emblem of the god of medicine. Poufs which paid tribute to the craze for hot-air ballooning (pouf à la*

Montgolfier) *and to French participation in the War of America Independence became popular, such as "liberty" and "the Philadelphia". French naval success in 1778 inspired over 20 new headdresses, including* La Belle Poule, *a picturesque coif with a miniature model of the famous frigate, complete with mast and guns, atop a scaffolding of almost two feet of hair.*

Marie Antoinette and Bertin enjoyed using fabric of unusual hues such as lavender, aquamarine, lemon yellow, violet and rose. In 1775, Marie Antoinette wore a gown that Louis XVI pronounced "the exact shade of a flea". Even unpleasant names were used: visitors laughed at fabrics called "Paris mud" or "dandies' intestines". After the birth of Marie Antoinette's son, a brown shade known as dauphin caca *came into vogue. Louis XVI ordered that locks of his wife's ash blonde hair be sent to the Gobelins factory and to Lyons so that tapestries and fabric could be made called* cheveux à la Reine.

By 1779, Bertin had reached the zenith of success. She employed 36 seamstresses and regularly sent large dolls dressed in her newest designs to all the courts of Europe.

In the 1780s, Marie Antoinette became concerned about her escalating wardrobe expenses. Although she still wore court dresses on state occasions, she began to dress in simpler fashions. They were made from cotton or muslin. Ironically, Bertin charged as much for simple clothes as for heavily decorated gowns made from yards of costly silk.

Bertin fell on hard times in 1785 and declared bankruptcy two years later. She refused to sever ties with the queen and in 1791 and 1792 Marie Antoinette ordered 40 poufs *and 50 bonnets from her in 19 months. Knowing she would probably never be paid, Bertin continued to make clothes for Marie Antoinette after the royal family was imprisoned. She sent mourning clothes and a black bonnet to the former queen after Louis XVI was guillotined.*

In 1792, during one of their last meetings, Marie Antoinette sadly told the modiste, *"I dreamed of you last night, dear Rose; I thought that you brought me many coloured ribbons, and that I chose several, but they all turned black as soon as I took them in my hands."*

WOMEN'S FASHION IN THE REIGN OF LOUIS XVI.

walls with delicate panels adorned with emblems personally relevant to the queen: Austrian eagles, peacocks (in 1775, Marie Antoinette launched the fashion of wearing peacock feathers in the hair), and dolphins, symbolizing the new Dauphin. Mique tucked a low daybed covered in ice-blue silk into a curtained alcove lined with mirrored panels to reflect the chandelier's flickering light. When the queen first peered into the alcove, she stood at an angle that made it appear as if her head was missing from her body. Marie Antoimette shrieked, then she and her ladies dissolved into laughter.

Every object in the *Méridienne* was designed to delight the queen and reflect her personal taste. Louis XVI made the room's gilded door locks in his private forge and installed them himself; decorated with his wife's monogram, they remain in place today. A musical clock that played her favourite melody sat on the table, and even the heads of favourite dogs had been carved into the armrests of her chairs. The queen passionately loved furniture and patronized the most gifted craftsmen and artists in Europe. She commissioned many exquisite pieces for her private rooms at Versailles, and her favourite furniture-maker, Reisener, crafted a delicate mechanical table for the *Méridienne* with gorgeous marquetry and costly gilded mounts. One push of a tiny button allowed secret drawers to spring open and reveal compartments where letters or cosmetics could be hidden. Reisener, German like many renowned cabinet-makers, began working as a purveyor to Marie Antoinette in 1771 and served as *ébéniste du Roi*.

Marie Antoinette continued to dress in her formal bedchamber where, according to tradition, her *lever* took place every morning, and countesses, princesses and duchesses assisted with the royal toilette by handing her a candlestick or chemise. As her gowns and headdresses became more elaborate, she wanted her favourite dressmaker, Rose Bertin, to adjust her ruffles and lace. Shopkeepers and other commoners could not attend the *lever* so, to circumvent this rule, Marie Antoinette changed the etiquette and gave Bertin entrée to the *petits appartements*. Soon, the queen left her bedroom after having her hair dressed and, without a backwards glance at the assembled group, disappeared through a hidden door beside the bed. Bertin, waiting in the *Méridienne*, would confer alone with her royal patron for hours as the queen admired herself in the many mirrors. Courtiers and guests stood impatiently, until Marie Antoinette, beribboned and beplumed, finally emerged. Rancour towards the queen soared and, by the 1780s, much of the nobility no longer cared to drive to Versailles to see an inaccessible monarch who preferred to spend time with an entourage of young friends or her purveyors.

Although both the king and queen used private cabinets at Versailles, Marie Antoinette entertained more. Louis's rooms contained a forge, carpentry room and a large library, his first addition to the château after becoming monarch. In 1775, he ordered a long secret corridor built to connect the queen's bedroom to the entresol of the *Salon de l'Oeil de Boeuf* in his apartments. The king's private rooms could be visited by anyone when he was out, but the public never toured the queen's rooms. English writer/agriculturalist Arthur Young travelled to Versailles in 1787 and recalled, "in viewing the king's apartment, which he had not left a quarter of an hour, with those slight traits of disorder that showed he lived in it, it was amusing to see the blackguard figures walking about the palace, and even in his bedchamber; men whose rags betrayed them to be in the last stage of poverty … I desired to see the queen's apartment, but I could not. 'Is Her Majesty in?' I asked. 'No,' was the reply. 'Why then not see it as well as the king's?' The answer came, 'Heavens, Monsieur, that is not done.'"

As her power and prestige grew after the birth of the Dauphin, Marie Antoinette added to her private apartments. Used during the previous reign by Louis XV's wife, these rooms overlooked a gloomy inner courtyard and since natural light rarely entered, the queen decorated with pale colours and airy fabrics. These salons and their accompanying boudoirs eventually spread over three floors, and the queen and her ladies bustled up and down labyrinthine corridors and steep, winding back stairs with thin handrails. The women discarded their wide hoopskirts for loose fitting gowns so that they could move quickly through the narrow hallways.

Although Marie Antoinette still slept in her official bedchamber, by the 1780s she spent most of her time in the private rooms, called the *cabinet intérieur de la Reine*. Hardly any dignitaries and courtiers saw these salons, which became the subject of much conjecture. The queen's rooms, entered by using concealed panels, remained hidden behind locked doors. Utterly different from Versailles' ostentatious public staterooms designed to awe, the elegant inner salons, where royalty actually lived, remained a secret world of elaborate *trompe'l'oeil* panels, small inner stairways, and doll-like furniture. These chambers were designed for privacy; the corners of some rooms had even been angled so that servants could pass through carrying firewood or water without disturbing the queen and her guests.

The arrangement of the queen's inner suite was so complicated that only a few trusted servants knew its entirety. The billiards room sat on the château's top floor. The décor was simple except for a set of armchairs made of gilded beech wood and covered in white embroidered silk; exquisite carved lilacs danced over the frames of these chairs, made by Georges Jacob. In 1787, the queen ordered her billiards room remade into a sitting room for the upper floor of her suite. Underneath lay the royal nursery with rooms for the children, their nurses and staff.

The main floor of the *petits appartements* was used daily by the queen. Almost every room held a dainty *table à écrire*, a writing table with graceful lines sometimes decorated with colourful Sèvres porcelain plaques; Marie Antoinette commissioned many pieces of porcelain-mounted furniture during the 1780s. The queen's bathing room lay near the *Méridienne*. Equipped with hot and cold running water, the room featured a slanted tiled floor for drainage and had an adjacent lounging area. Marie Antoinette, known for her modesty, wore a long flannel shift while bathing in her copper tub and sometimes ate a light meal while relaxing in the perfumed water. At the end of her bath, her

QUEEN OF THE COIFFURE

In 1776, elaborate feathered headdresses, some reaching as high as three feet, became the vogue at Versailles. This craze lasted four years, and the price of heron and peacock plumes skyrocketed. No one's headdress was higher than Marie Antoinette's, and one observer noted that, "when the queen passed along the gallery at Versailles, you could see nothing but a forest of feathers, rising a foot-and-a-half above the head, and nodding to and fro." When her brother, Emperor Joseph II, visited from Austria in 1777, he mocked this frivolity by labelling her "featherbrained". Madame Campan wrote that, due to the height of these creations, ladies suddenly found the roof of their carriage too low and were forced to either put their heads out of the window or to ride in a kneeling position.

Elaborate headdresses were worn atop wigs, or a combination of real and artificial hair that had been crimped, curled, teased, frizzed and braided into an enormous mountain. Often a horsehair cone sat atop the head, with a lady's hair brushed up to completely hide it. The bouffant creation would then be pomaded and powdered white or grey using huge powder puffs or bellows. Ribbons, gauze, wreaths, flowers, pearls and diamonds wound around these massive confections, which were kept intact as long as possible. During the 1700s, washing hair was considered risky as water near the head and brain was thought to cause illness. Many elegant ladies of Versailles complained of fleas in their towering edifices; itches were remedied by using a special long-handled ivory headscratcher. The coiffures were given outlandish names: the "sleeping dog", "the royal bird", "the cradle of love", "the mountain of desire". Crowns of real flowers were worn tucked into tiny bottles of water shaped like the curvature of the head and concealed in the hair so that the blooms would last through a long ball followed by supper. Marie Antoinette, always on the forefront of fashion, wore such elaborate hair-dos that courtiers joked she was "queen of the coiffure" even before she became queen of France.

Léonard Autié, Marie Antoinette's official hairdresser, began working for her soon after she arrived in France. He designed fetching curls that hid her unusually high, wide forehead. Everyone at court agreed that the result was pure magic and, breaking with tradition, she encouraged him to continue with other clients so he would be attuned to the latest Parisian fads; until then, the queen's hairdresser worked exclusively for her. Léonard's styles, worn for over a decade, included: the coiffure à la dauphine, *with hair rolled into long sausage curls that spilled onto the shoulders. The voluble* coiffeur *bragged that Marie Antoinette's head measured a full 72 inches from the top of the hair to the bottom of the chin when she wore his* coiffure loge d'opéra, *introduced in 1772; this saucy headdress was decorated with three large feathers, a bow of pink ribbon and a large precious stone, usually a ruby.*

Léonard replaced women's caps with strips of gauze and other light fabric woven into the hair to add volume, which became very popular. He prided himself on having invented the sentimental pouf, *which incorporated personal items unique to a lady's life into her tresses. His most famous creation in this style was for the Duchesse de Chartres in 1774: her profusion of hair included a miniature parrot eating a cherry, her son being rocked by his nurse, a replica of a young African servant and hair from her husband, father and child. Butterflies, cupids, and favourite pets paraded across heads, and the birth of the Dauphin was commemorated in many hairstyles.*

Marie Antoinette's blonde tresses began to fall out after her son's birth. Since she was no longer able to wear the towering coiffures she adored, Léonard invented a hairstyle called à l'enfant, *which consisted of one long curl cascading down the shoulder. A reliable confidante, Léonard knew the queen's secrets; she entrusted him to carry her jewels to safekeeping during the Revolution.*

attendants held large towels so that her body remained hidden from view. In cold weather, the queen used a portable hipbath rolled near the fireplace. She used an English-style water closet, or toilet, which was a novelty at Versailles.

Although Marie Antoinette had two well-stocked libraries in her *petits appartements*, she preferred singing or playing the harp to literature. Her jaded friend Monsieur de Besenval, who became one of the queen's favourite male companions during the 1770s and 1780s, wrote that she avoided intellectual activity and, "apart from a few novels, never opened a book." She liked having plays read to her, particularly the controversial works of Beaumarchais.

Her first library was constructed during the early 1770s and redone in 1781. This small room featured tall doors concealed by a high *trompe-l'oeil* panel depicting rows of hand-painted faux books bearing bookmarks of real satin ribbon. This library, mostly white accented with vivid pale green fabric and gold framing, held rows of books stretching from the parquet floor to the high ceiling. The gilded shelves were adjustable, and there were ornate drawer pulls shaped as imperial eagles, a reminder of the queen's Austrian heritage. The court bookbinder covered each volume in red morocco and had Marie Antoinette's emblem, three fleurs-de-lis, hand-tooled on the front. Her personal librarian, Monsieur Campan, organized her collection, although many books were used solely as decoration. Her second library, smaller and decorated in blue, had less natural light and was used for larger volumes.

A difficult patron, Marie Antoinette had little understanding of the expenses or problems caused by her demands. Discussion of the lack of money in the building funds allotted for her projects could send her into a fury. When she began expanding her *petits cabinets*, she wanted ornate carved bookcases in several rooms. When she saw the plain ones purchased in an attempt to save money, she insisted they be removed in her presence and new ones ordered. To the dismay of architects and designers, the queen frequently changed her mind. In the late 1780s, annoyed by noisy guards in the courtyard below her private rooms, she took possession of a new ground floor suite looking onto the main courtyard. She gave orders to destroy a library in these rooms and quickly build a new bathroom and workmen laboured until almost dawn tearing out plaster. A few hours later, a new command arrived from Marie Antoinette insisting that the old walls must be kept. "It's enough to make you go crazy," wrote the aggravated architect Jean-François Heurtier. The resulting *appartement des bains*, designed by Mique, still exists and is decorated with panels with white carvings of lobsters, shells, tridents, dolphins and water pouring from vases.

In 1783, Marie Antoinette wanted a private audience room added to her inner apartments and asked that a cabinet built during the reign of Louis XIV be redone in a style then called "return to antiquity". An early Neoclassical delight, this white salon, the largest of the queen's private rooms, was renamed the *cabinet doré* (Gilded Cabinet). It held eight panels decorated with gilt carvings of winged sphinxes and smoking incense-burners; the excavation of Pompeii and Herculaneum inspired these decorations. The queen enjoyed sitting by the dark-red marble fireplace, decorated with female caryatids, and organizing her knick-knacks: Japanese lacquer, pietra dure, blue porcelain from China, petrified wood, and pieces of rock crystal. She displayed over 70 pieces from her collection in this room.

Dressed in Rose Bertin's latest creation, Marie Antoinette relaxed in the *cabinet doré* by plucking the strings of her harp as she waited for a scratch at the door to announce a visitor; at Versailles, a knock was considered uncouth, and staff scraped the door with a pinkie nail before entering. She sat for many portraits by her favourite painter, Vigée Lebrun, in this room and received visits from the great composer Christoph Gluck, her music instructor in Vienna. She met her intimate friends here, including Axel Fersen, a handsome Swedish count rumoured to be her lover. The queen preferred to dine in her private apartments, especially on Sundays when the *grand couvert* was laid. Louis XVI never minded eating in public, according to tradition, but Marie Antoinette hated being watched while she ate. She felt embarrassed about the vast quantities eaten by the king, and how his subjects noticed his sloppy manners.

MARIE ANTOINETTE AND HER CHILDREN,
A PORTRAIT BY THE QUEEN'S FAVOURED ARTIST,
VIGÉE-LEBRUN.
akg-images

THE QUEEN'S FAVOURITE PAINTER

Marie Antoinette commissioned portraits and art from dozens of sculptors and painters but was best known for her patronage of Elisabeth Louise Vigée-Lebrun (1755–1842) who began working at Versailles in the late 1770s copying existing portraits of the queen. In 1778, she painted Marie Antoinette from life for the first time. Vigée-Lebrun, known for her beauty and charm, was the same age as the queen, and the two women enjoyed each other's company, regularly singing duets in the cabinet doré.

Vigée-Lebrun recalled the queen's kindness when, nearing the end of pregnancy, she missed a sitting. "I hastened to Versailles the next day to offer my excuses. The queen was not expecting me; she had her horses harnessed to go out driving. The chamberlain received me with a stiff, haughty manner, and bellowed, 'It was yesterday, Madame, that Her Majesty expected you …' Upon my reply that I had simply come to take her orders for another day, he went to the queen, who at once had me conducted to her room. She was holding a book in her hand, hearing her daughter repeat a lesson. My heart was beating violently, as I knew that I was in the wrong. But the queen looked up at me and said, in a friendly voice, 'I waited for you all morning yesterday; what happened to you?' I replied, 'I am sorry to say that I was ill … I am here to receive your orders, and then I will immediately leave.' 'No, No! Do not go!" exclaimed the queen. 'I do not want you to have made your journey for nothing.'" She cancelled her drive and gave a sitting to the painter. Flustered at Marie Antoinette's thoughtfulness, Vigée-Lebrun then dropped her pencils and brushes on the floor. She bent to gather them, but the queen quickly said, "Never mind, you are too advanced with child to stoop," and picked them up herself.

Vigée-Lebrun often painted the queen holding a rose, the symbol of love and beauty and encouraged Marie Antoinette to dress more informally.

THE MARIE ANTOINETTE BALLOON

Aviation pioneers Joseph and Etienne Montgolfier, brothers from a small town near Lyons, launched the first hot-air balloon in Paris in 1783. The Montgolfier brothers received funding from the Royal government and were eager to send up a manned ballon but, as the effects of higher altitude on man were unknown, the king insisted that a test be made using animals.

On 19 September 1785 Louis XVI, Marie Antoinette, their court, and 100,000 spectators gathered at Versailles in the château's forecourt to watch the Montgolfiers' experiment. A sheep, rooster and duck were placed in a large cage attached to an elaborately-decorated royal blue and gold montgolfière, the balloon's new name. They took off through a thick cloud of dark smoke and travelled about two miles during their eight-minute flight before landing safely.

Other aviators quickly followed with aeronautic experiments. Parisians watched balloons take off from all over the city and these events were commemorated in clocks, engravings and furniture. In 1784, Marie Antoinette commissioned a pair of side chairs from George Jacob with balloon-shaped finials for the château des Tuileries; one of these chairs is now owned by the Metropolitan Museum of Art in New York City.

Benjamin Franklin witnessed a manned flight in Paris on 1 December 1783. He left a vivid description, "Being a little indisposed, and the air cool, and the ground damp, I declined going into the garden of the Tuileries, where the balloon was placed, not knowing how long I might be obliged to wait… and chose to stay in my carriage near the statue of Louis XV [in today's Place de la Concorde], from whence I could well see it rise… All Paris was out, either about the Tuileries, on the quays and bridges, in the fields, the streets, at the windows, or on the tops of houses… Between one and two o'clock, all eyes were gratified with seeing it rise majestically from among the trees, and ascend gradually above the buildings, a most beautiful spectacle. When it was about two hundred feet high, the brave adventurers held out and waved a little white pennant, on both sides of their car, to salute the spectators, who returned loud claps of applause." While watching the ascent, an observer turned to the famous American statesman/inventor and cynically asked, "But what good is a balloon?" Franklin thought for a moment, then replied: "What good is a newborn baby?"

The following year, King Gustav III of Sweden visited France and, as part of the festivities, a balloon was launched in his honour at Versailles. The queen allowed her name to be used and, on 23 June 1784 the Marie Antoinette montgolfière ascended over the château. Decorated with Louis XVI's and Gustavus III's ciphers, this balloon, the largest to date, remained aloft for 45 minutes before landing at Chantilly.

QUEEN MARIE ANTOINETTE AND LOUIS XVI AT THE HUNT,
BY LOUIS AUGUSTE BRUN.
Collection of the author.

CHÂTEAU DE FONTAINEBLEAU

FRENCH RULERS VISITED THE MAGNIFICENT RENAISSANCE CHÂTEAU OF FONTAINEBLEAU EVERY AUTUMN TO HUNT WILD ANIMALS IN THE SURROUNDING FOREST. DURING THE *VOYAGE DE FONTAINEBLEAU*, which usually lasted six weeks, the court migrated from Versailles at great expense. The Royal Furniture Warehouse in Paris (see Other Places, page 152) sent tapestries, rugs, desks and chairs to the château, and hundreds of wagons with furniture and heavy trunks rolled into the palace's courtyards. Over 2,000 horses, not counting those for baggage, transported the royal family and courtiers; Marie Antoinette sometimes went to Fontainebleau by yacht if pregnant or ill.

Although the château lodged 176 functionaries, Louis XVI's court consisted of around 250; those not allotted space in the château rented a room at inns. The king's guests expected to be entertained, and Marie Antoinette held lavish masked ballets and masquerade balls. On Tuesdays, Thursdays and Saturdays, performers from the Comédie-Française presented shows with elaborate costumes and sets. On other evenings, light operas were held or dancers and comedians amused the court. Louis XVI rarely attended these shows. He chose to go to bed early and rise before dawn to prepare for *la chasse*, the traditional pastime of Bourbon monarchs. Although he liked shooting and killed as many as 200 wild birds in an outing, he preferred stag hunting which he tried to fit into his schedule several times a week. The king recorded statistics for each hunt with a diligence bordering on fanaticism; he daily noted how many animals had been shot, of what kind, and where.

Louis insisted on perpetuating the hunting traditions of his ancestors: participants wore costumes and the braiding of each uniform indicated which animal the wearer could hunt. Ambassadors and distinguished guests

VISITING FONTAINEBLEAU

During the Revolution, royal châteaux were stripped of their furnishings, which were sold at public auction. Fontainebleau sat empty until the early 1800s, when Napoleon redid many ceremonial rooms and private apartments. During the early 1800s, Empress Josephine used Marie Antoinette's Salon des Jeux, and the room is now sometimes called the Empress's Grand Salon. Josephine fell in love with Marie Antoinette's boudoir and kept the room as it was originally decorated. The boudoir and the Salon des Jeux can be seen during the tour of the Private Apartments [contact Fontainebleau for dates and times of tour].

Fontainebleau, 35 miles southeast of Paris, is approximately an hour's train ride from the Gare de Lyon. At the Fontainebleau station, take the bus marked "Château" (another five miles). The SNCF sells one ticket for both the train and bus. The Musée National du Château de Fontainebleau is open: Wednesday, Thursday, Friday, Saturday, Sunday and Monday from 9.30 am – 6.00 pm (June to September); from 9.30 am – 5.00 pm (October to May). Much of the château can be seen in a self-guided tour, and there are audio guides in English. However, Marie Antoinette's boudoir in the private apartments can only be seen in small, guided groups.

often attended, and the king continued his grandfather's custom of holding private suppers after the hunt. The menu boasted the monarch's favourites: paté and cutlets with fresh vegetables, usually green beans and artichokes.

While Marie Antoinette disliked living far from Paris and its diversions, she loved the euphoria she felt while racing through the forest following the chase. As hunting often led to accidents two equerries accompanied her with a small army of pages, grooms, and postilions close by. As Dauphine, she followed the hunters in a calèche filled with refreshments so she and her ladies could picnic with the sportsmen. As the royal buglers played fanfares, she nibbled on roast duck, mingled with laughing young people, and appreciated the relaxed etiquette of the outdoor life.

Though her mother insisted long hours in the saddle led to miscarriage, Marie Antoinette soon abandoned her calèche for horse riding. To her husband's delight, she began to follow the hunt on a light grey stallion outfitted with an embroidered blue or scarlet velvet caparison. Soon the queen galloped through the woods as English hounds, spaniels and other dogs dashed alongside. The royal couple grew closer as they shared a mutual love of riding.

Marie Antoinette felt the king appeared at his best on horseback dressed in the uniform of the royal hunt: a blue and crimson jacket with velvet cuffs, tight breeches, and tall leather boots with a funnel type top. She adored the simpler clothes worn outdoors. Men's riding clothes heavily influenced the cut of female riding attire, and the queen found this masculine, English-style tailoring flattering to her figure. In November 1781, she gave proof of this affinity by ordering 31 velvet or silk riding outfits. Many had tight-waisted jackets with a matching skirt and buttoned waistcoat similar to those popular among the British aristocracy.

Pleased with her appearance in riding clothes, Marie Antoinette commissioned a portrait of herself as a horsewoman as a gift for her mother. This pastel, by Joseph Krantzinger in 1771, depicted the Dauphine wearing a three cornered hat, gold braided riding habit with buttoned waistcoat and holding a riding whip. Over a decade later,

LE JEU DU ROI AFTER CHARLES NICHOLAS COCHIN.

Louis-Auguste Brun (1758–1815) painted the queen riding sidesaddle dressed in a blue satin riding dress and plumed hat. The king, also on horseback, watches her with a satisfied expression from the background. Like most German princesses, Marie Antoinette did not grow up riding sidesaddle, and in another portrait, Brun portrayed her astride a spirited dark stallion. The queen wore a gold and green riding suit topped with a jaunty hat decorated with white and black plumes. A white muslin cravat matched the long sash knotted at her waist; leather boots with a high rounded heel, grey riding gloves and whip completed her ensemble. Even her little gold stirrups were exquisitely ornate.

Although Louis XVI and Marie Antoinette regularly visited Fontainebleau, they did not undertake major remodelling until the the 1780s. The king then requested alterations to his apartments and, at the same time, Marie Antoinette commissioned the architect Pierre-Marie Rousseau to redo her private chambers. Two of the rooms constructed for the queen around 1785 can be toured today and are considered extraordinary examples of eighteenth-century French decorative arts: her private boudoir and the *Salon des Jeux*, where she gambled in public.

The *Salon des Jeux*, or Queen's Game Room, was whimsically decorated with stucco caducei and winged hats, symbols of Mercury, the god of gamblers and thievery. Marie Antoinette played cards for hours under this room's elaborately painted ceiling depicting Minerva crowning the Muses. Her small crimson gaming purse embroidered with three fleurs-de-lis lay in her lap as she gambled at a felt-topped table while the room's many candles burned down to their wicks. The queen's love of antiquity caused Rousseau to decorate the top of each door with sphinxes and fill the room with other Egyptian motifs. The *Salon des Jeux* held tables used in 13 different types of games including lotto, three-of-a-kind, piquet, quadrille, and backgammon. Spectators knelt on *voyeuses*, low chairs designed for observing card games; the viewer straddled the seat and used its back as an elbow rest. After becoming a mother, Marie Antoinette tried to cut back on her gambling and held concerts and formal audiences in this room.

GAMBLING

As a girl in Austria, Marie Antoinette often watched card-games and lotteries played at court for higher stakes than in France. Although Bourbon royalty traditionally played cards in public, these games, lansquenet and cavagnol, were only held on important occasions and little money changed hands. After becoming queen, Marie Antoinette became obsessed by the jeu and played in public three times a week. Anyone who could afford the stakes could sit at the same table as the queen, who sometimes found herself with partners who had no title. Faro, a risky game where losses mounted quickly, became her favourite, and the queen liked to play for such high stakes that courtiers gladly let strangers take their place at her table. Although Marie Antoinette was never accused of dishonesty, some ladies cheated, and the queen often lost heavily and had to ask her husband to pay her debts. Louis XVI disliked games of chance and reckless spending and placed limits on betting, although Marie Antoinette begged him to change his mind.

To celebrate her twenty-first birthday, she asked Louis to allow professional card players to come from Paris for an evening of gambling. He agreed with the stipulation that this would be a one-time event. To his dismay, the game continued for 36 hours, although the queen did not participate continuously. In blatant disregard of etiquette and religion, the players kept gambling well into the morning of All Saints Day. When her pious husband reproached her, Marie Antoinette impishly replied that, since he had not set a fixed length to the game, the fault was his. The king laughed and allowed her to participate in another all-night gambling session the following month. Her frenzied behaviour led Mercy to write, "Her game has become very expensive. She no longer plays ordinary games in which losses are limited… Her ladies and courtiers are frightened and hurt by the losses which they incur in order to pay court to the queen." When scolded by her mother's ambassador, Marie Antoinette asked him, "What should I do? There is nothing I dread as much as boredom."

The queen's tiny hand-painted boudoir, considered the most exquisite of Marie Antoinette's salons still in existence, resembled a fantasy more than a room. Rousseau chose the pearl as the theme for the décor, and the boudoir sparkled with gold, silver, and iridescent mother of pearl. Although only used one season (1786), this intimate boudoir became legendary for the synergy between its décor and extraordinary furniture, designed to match the room's wainscoting and fireplace. Jean-Henri Riesener designed the queen's roll-top desk and sewing table, made from steel and gilded bronze mounts over a mother of pearl veneer. Riesener built a matching sewing table so Marie Antoinette, who embroidered to relax, could chat with a friend *tête à tête* while completing needlework. Considered the royal cabinetmaker's finest work, both pieces were lost during the Revolution and did not reappear until the early 1960s. Graceful armchairs by George Jacob covered in silk brocade completed the boudoir's décor.

Only the queen's intimate circle visited her here. Motifs derived from ancient Pompeii covered the walls, and detailed sculptures of the Muses rested atop each door. Cleverly placed mirrors above the fireplace and around the room maximized natural light from a window to make the boudoir appear larger. Even the white marble fireplace delighted visitors with its allusions to archery: the mantle, decoratively embellished with a bronze bow surrounded by garlands, was supported on either side by a long quiver holding feather-tipped golden arrows. Rousseau grasped the queen's love of neoclassical lines and interpreted them through a theme of the pearl.

Although Marie Antoinette kept the formal Queen's Bedchamber as used by her predecessors, she commissioned new doors of mahogany and gold with elaborately carved overdoors of golden figures on a lapis-lazuli background. Today the walls are decorated with an exact replica of the colourful silk wall hangings made in Lyon for Marie Antoinette's use in this room. She ordered the huge ceremonial bed seen here today, but never used it as, in 1786, Louis XVI made the difficult decision to discontinue annual visits to Fontainebleau in an effort to economize.

RAMBOUILLET.

Collection of the author.

AS FRANCE'S FINANCES WORSENED IN THE EARLY 1780S, LOUIS XVI'S GOVERNMENT DESCENDED INTO A BUREAUCRATIC MORASS. THINGS WERE NOT GOING WELL; NOT ONLY DID THE KING'S MINISTERS lack the vision and skills needed to implement necessary economic reforms, none of them told the monarch how desperate the fiscal crisis had become.

Expenditures mounted as the court continued to move from one royal residence to another. Besides hunting at Fontainebleau, Louis enjoyed *la chasse* at Rambouillet, a dense forest to the southwest of Versailles, but if he hunted there late into the day, he and his retinue had no place to sleep. In late 1783, the king purchased the château of Rambouillet from a relative, Louis de Bourbon (1725–1793), the Duc de Penthièvre, in order to use it for a hunting lodge. The château itself dated from the 1300s and, although lavishly decorated, could not begin to hold the administrative machinery of Louis's court. Construction quickly began on a building for 400 officials that would connect to the château by a long underground passage. The king insisted that stables for 500 horses be built, as well as kennels, and a pheasant house. Hoping to improve the quality of French wool, Louis XVI had developed an interest in sheep breeding. He began work on an experimental farm at Rambouillet and, in 1786, bought 359 prized Merino rams and ewes, and had them transported to Rambouillet. Coveted for their luxurious wool, this was the first time that Merino sheep had been allowed to leave Spain. These became the ancestors for virtually all of today's prized Rambouillet sheep; the fine wool from the descendants of these unusually large animals is still highly sought after.

BREAST CUPS AND CHINA

Marie Antoinette often ate light meals in the dairy at Rambouillet, usually with her husband's younger sister Elisabeth. The queen had ordered a special set of whimsical, hand-painted china for the diary from Sèvres, the royal porcelain workshops. Few pieces of the original service exist, and this china is now among the world's most expensive porcelain.

Marie Antoinette selected over 65 pieces of china from Sèvres in various shades of ice blue, burgundy, violet, and yellow over a cream-coloured base. Some bowls and cups rested on tripod bases of goats' heads or cow's legs, while other pieces were painted with geometric figures and Etruscan designs and matched the dairy's sandstone exterior. The pieces used most frequently included jugs, butter dishes, sugar bowls, and large decorative faux-wooden milk pails used as centrepieces. The most unusual items were jattes teton, *breast bowls inspired by Greek mastos cups used around the sixth century BC. These large cups, shaped like a woman's breast and used for drinking milk, rested on a tripod of goats' heads and feet. A life-like nipple sat at the bottom of the bowl. Gossip spread that Marie Antoinette's own breast was the model for these bowls.*

Some original pieces of the queen's dairy service can be seen at the Musée national de ceramique at Sèvres [see Other Places, page 156], and the Metropolitan Museum of Art in New York owns a bowl. Ancienne Manufacture Royale has reissued these distinctive breast cups and several other unusual pieces from the service [see Shops, page 158].

Vivant Denon, engraver and future director of museums for Napoleon, sold his collection of 525 Etruscan and Greek vases and other pottery to Louis XVI in 1786. The king sent them to Sèvres to be used as models. Many pieces for the queen's dairy service were copied from Denon's collection. Sèvres made few dairy services during the 1700s, although many French and British estates had pleasure dairies.

In November 1783, Marie Antoinette visited Rambouillet to see her husband's new acquisition, pronounced it "odious," and asked, "What am I supposed to do in this gothic toad hole?" Her three-room suite overlooked the garden, which she found gloomy. Even her boudoir, still intact, with hand-carved oak panels, depressed her.

In an effort to make his wife want to visit Rambouillet, Louis XVI decided to have a surprise built for her in the English garden: a tiny exquisite pleasure dairy (*laiterie d'agrément*) similar to one he had seen while visiting his cousin, the Prince de Condé, at Chantilly. The king asked celebrated landscape artist Hubert Robert, who had already been commissioned to redo Rambouillet's gardens, to secretly design this dairy. Robert, working with Jacques-Jean Thévenin, envisioned an austere, stylishly sparse temple of cream-coloured stone. The interior would have only two rooms – one round, one rectangular – but would be filled with opulent, elegant decor. Although no one knew it at the time, this dairy at Rambouillet, created by some of France's finest designers, architects, painters, sculptors, china and furniture makers, became one of the last important artistic creations of the *Ancien Régime*.

On 20 June 1786 Louis escorted the queen to a nearby garden where a curtain of branches had been hung between two pavilions. When Louis gave a signal, workers threw aside the curtain, showing the queen her new plaything.

Beaming, Marie Antoinette approached the dairy. She could see the its inner rooms as she stepped between the Tuscan columns on either side of the front door. The first room she entered, intended as a tasting room, held waist-high counters of Carrara marble that encircled the walls and were meant for a collection of vases and porcelain bowls used for milk and cheese. A domed ceiling adorned with rose-like ornaments topped this circular lounge.

The dusky inner room, the rectangular *Pièce de Fraicheur*, or cool room, held small fountains used to cool milk. Fresh water gushed into basins ensuring that the dairy would not be hot even on a summer day. At one end of this room, Robert placed a romantic grotto with large rocks stacked from floor to ceiling. This grotto held the dairy's

THE ENGLISH GARDEN

Long canals stretched from the château into the park and, at the eastern end of the canals, the Duc de Penthièvre, commissioned a lush Jardin Anglais *for his daughter-in-law, the Princesse de Lamballe, who was the queen's close friend. Even though the English garden was far from the château, Marie Antoinette regarded it as the estate's redeeming feature. Built in 1779, the garden was filled with quaint winding paths and unusual statues. A Chinese kiosk sat atop a manmade mountain, and the* princesse *adored the tiny fairy-tale cottage with thatched roof. Inside was a breathtaking salon called the* Chaumière des Coquillages *that took years to complete; it sparkled with countless delicate seashells, pearls, and glass that had been carefully embedded in its walls. The* princesse *also had a tiny boudoir, delicately decorated with hand-painted flowers and singing birds. When two cabinets were opened, mechanical dolls in African costumes presented perfume and face powder.*

VISITING RAMBOUILLET

Trains usually depart from Paris's Gare Montparnasse for la Gare de Rambouillet every 20 minutes daily. The château, 34 miles southwest of Paris, is the summer home of the President of the Republic and can be toured when he is not in residence. The Laiterie de la Reine, *Marie Antoinette's dairy, lies approximately half a mile from the château in the estate's park. Both château and dairy are open daily except Tuesdays and holidays. The château's hours are: April to September Wednesday to Monday, 10.00 to 11.45 am and 2.00 to 5.00 pm; October to March Wednesday to Monday, 10.00 to 11.45 am and 2.00 to 4.00 pm. The dairy's hours are: Summer: 10.00 to 12.00, 2.00 to 5.30 pm – Winter: 10.00 to 12.00, 2.00 to 3.30 pm. For more information, call the Rambouillet tourist office at 01 34 83 21 21.*

artistic centrepiece: *La Chevrière,* an exquisite white marble statue by Pierre Julien of the nymph Amalthea with the goat that suckled the god Zeus as an infant, a reference to Ovid's timeless story. A cleverly placed skylight illuminated the statue and the mythological bas-reliefs around the room that glowed like windows in the dark. Julien (1731–1804), a renowned artist who executed all sculpture at the dairy, completed the grotto's decoration with mythological bas-reliefs. A relief over the door depicted a mother suckling her baby, and a white marble floor completed the décor. Julien filled the dairy with carvings that would please the queen, who is supposed to have smiled when she saw the inscription above the outer door, which read *la Laiterie de la Reine* (the Queen's Dairy).

Furniture and porcelain did not arrive until late the following spring. Hubert Robert designed the décor to compliment the dairy's neoclassical exterior. He sketched armchairs, milking stools, and tables like those used in ancient times, which were then handcrafted from mahogany by George Jacob. Twenty-five pieces, decorated with carved Egyptian palmetto leaves and ram's heads, were ordered for the dairy, along with orange seat cushions bordered in black. Goat and ram motifs, used throughout, were continued in the decoration of the dairy's china, made by Sèvres for the dairy. Enjoying fresh milk and cheese had become the vogue in the French court, and the queen and her guests gathered here to banter while nibbling fruit, cheese, or ice cream. Since there was no barn for cows or rooms designed for churning butter or making cheese, this *laiterie* was used for entertaining rather than as a working dairy.

Hubert Robert planted rare trees in the park surrounding the dairy. Red oaks and cypress trees from America, exotic plants, and unusual shrubbery were used to soften the building's austere neoclassical lines.

In April 1787, Louis XVI, now aware that his government was nearly bankrupt, told the Comte de Brienne that if he had known the extent of France's debts he would never have purchased Rambouillet. His last trip to the château was in August of the next year, and Marie Antoinette did not visit after the summer of 1787.

THE QUEEN'S HAMEAU AND ARTIFICIAL LAKE AT VERSAILLES.

Collection of the author.

DRAMA QUEEN: THE THEATRE AND HAMEAU
AT THE PETIT TRIANON

Would you know
A cuckold, a whore, a bastard?
See the King, the Queen
And Monsieur the Dauphin…

SO WENT A POPULAR TUNE SUNG IN PARIS DURING THE 1780S. AS FRANCE CAREENED TOWARDS REVOLUTION, ILLUSTRATED LAMPOONS AND PORNOGRAPHIC PAMPHLETS WITH LEWD ENGRAVINGS gleefully portrayed Louis XVI as impotent and Marie Antoinette as an Austrian nymphomaniac. She was held responsible for unpopular decisions made by the king, though she had little political power. Wildly inflated stories of her extravagance circulated through the kingdom, especially in the capital where all blame for emptying the treasury fell on selfish *Madame Déficit*, the Parisians' nickname for their queen. She now avoided the city that had held her in thrall only a few years earlier. Disillusioned with gambling and fashion, she sought solace in make-believe and built an expensive theatre and tiny village in the Petit Trianon park. Both still stand, relics from a world swept away by political and social upheaval.

Although the French nobility had enjoyed performing in private theatricals for decades, this popular pastime escalated during the 1780s. Tiny playhouses were built within mansions so that invited audiences could watch

WHAT CAN BE SEEN TODAY

Marie Antoinette's hameau *originally consisted of 12 buildings; 10 of them remain, including the Queen's House (the largest cottage, shown below), the mill with paddle wheel, the* réchauffoir, *the pigeon loft, and the Marlborough tower. The* hameau *is a half hour walk from the Petit Trianon. Although the cottages are not usually open to the public, visitors can walk around the grounds and artificial lake. Louis XVI suggested that a tiny* arc de Triomphe *be built at the far end of the* hameau. *Called the Porte Saint-Antoine, it still marks the north entrance to the park. The queen's farm, rebuilt in 1958, lies across the tree-lined Allée de Saint-Antoine, the avenue in front of the arch.*

The queen's theatre has been completely restored but is only open to the public intermittently. The building is a short walk from the Petit Trianon; ask there for directions to see the exterior.

nobles performing comedies or operettas. Marie Antoinette, who had grown up participating in amateur theatricals in Austria, threw herself into this new amusement. She spent hours memorizing lines and rehearsing with a small troupe of acting enthusiasts assembled from the royal family, including the king's younger brother and sister, the Comte d'Artois and Madame Elisabeth. The Duchesse de Polignac, who in 1782 was given the lucrative position of Governess to the Royal Children, participated, as did other friends. They studied with professional actors, and the queen took diction and acting lessons from a lauded Parisian thespian.

Although plays were regularly performed at Versailles, Marie Antoinette wanted her troupe to appear in its own theatre. With the king's consent, she commissioned architect Richard Mique to erect a freestanding hall solely for her use. She instructed the architect to design the interior to resemble the Opera at Versailles and asked that the dimensions exactly match those of another royal theatre at Choisy so scenery could be easily switched between venues.

Construction lasted about a year. On 1 June 1780, the queen's theatre was inaugurated with a programme of ballets and plays performed by actors from the Comédie-Française and Comédie-Italienne in Paris. The royal family and a few friends gathered at the Petit Trianon, and then strolled along a covered walkway to the new building. Its exterior appeared deceptively simple; the only adornment was an exquisite sculpture over the door of the queen's entrance of a pixie playing a lyre. As guests entered the candle-lit hall, many remarked that it was like stepping into a fantasy. Two galleries and spacious boxes filled the horseshoe-shaped hall, and the lush interior glimmered with gold. The curtain, seats, and wall hangings, made from velvet, silk and mohair, were a bright celestial blue. Above the proscenium, hand-painted to resemble veined white marble, a pair of bronze goddesses supported a glittering garland of fruit and flowers surrounding the queen's initials. A delicate painting of Apollo with the Muses and Graces adorned the ceiling, and blazing candelabras held by huge female figures spilled light onto the stage.

Two months after the inauguration of her new toy, Marie Antoinette felt ready to make her debut on the Trianon stage. Although the audience was strictly limited to the king and royal family, elaborate scenery had been constructed, and Rose Bertin hired to design costumes. At the last minute, Marie Antoinette decided that she and the other actors would perform with enthusiasm if there were more spectators and quickly filled the auditorium with 40 ladies-in-waiting, readers and ushers from her staff.

When courtiers learned that Marie Antoinette's servants had attended a play to which they had not been invited, many began to portray her as a royal *bête noire* who tinkered with tradition that, to them, was as sacrosanct as a nun's habit. Citing precedent from the days of Louis XIV and XV, they fruitlessly applied for admission. Inured to these requests, the queen replied intemperately that, as regards to her private fetes, she would invite whom she pleased. Outraged, the courtiers, usually ingratiating to the point of banality, erupted with anger. They even criticized her for allowing Richard Mique, who lived in a small apartment above the theatre, to attend a performance.

The Austrian ambassador, Comte de Mercy, initially felt the queen's desire to act with her friends was harmless. He wrote, "The time necessary to learn their parts and the rehearsals will keep them all out of mischief and gambling." Soon the ambassador changed his mind, and commented, "This kind of amusement restricted to such a few people becomes a marked sign of favour for those included, and a cause of jealousy and protest among the many who are left out." He added, "All such protests have had no effect and been the source of mortification; this has given rise to talk, which has spread from Versailles to Paris."

Marie Antoinette's choice of characters to portray on stage could not have been further from her station in life. She confided to her sister, "People think it very easy to play the queen – they are wrong. The constraints are endless, it seems that to be natural is a crime." She never chose to act the part of royalty, but pretended to be a peasant's wife, chambermaid, farmer's daughter, or village maiden. While on stage, the queen ironed and performed other menial tasks while dressed in simple, but flattering, costumes. Although some audience members said privately that watching her act was more exhausting than entertaining, the king found her performances appealing and clapped loudly when the fledgling actress delivered speeches or made a dramatic exit. His robust laugh filled the theatre when she delivered an amusing line, and he often visited her simple dressing room, still in existence, between scenes.

Although Marie Antoinette did not perform for visiting royalty, she invited them to her private theatre to hear operas by popular composers such as Salieri, Grétry and Gluck. The queen instructed that special librettos be printed and bound in leather with gold tooling as souvenirs for the royal family and special guests. Her theatre was frequently used during the early 1780s, and acting filled the queen's summers in 1780, 1782 and 1783. Performances halted with her pregnancy the following year but, in the summer of 1785, she decided to resume acting. The role she chose was Rosine, an effervescent, impudent beauty in *The Barber of Seville* by Pierre-Augustin Caron de Beaumarchais, whose work the king had banned.

Louis XVI detested Beaumarchais's writing. After hearing a soliloquy from his most famous play *The Marriage of Figaro* in which the nobility was asked, "What have you done to have so much good fortune? You took the trouble to be born and nothing more," the usually tolerant monarch growled, "This man undermines everything that should be respected in government."

Although aware her husband had forbidden performances of Beaumarchais's work, Marie Antoinette was determined to play Rosine and pressured the king until he allowed her to stage *The Barber of Seville*. She made elaborate plans for this production to be the finest ever presented at her theatre with inventive scenery and endless costume changes. She enlisted the king's brother, Artois, to play the famous part of Figaro, the witty barber-surgeon.

THE DIAMOND NECKLACE AFFAIR

In 1778, knowing of Marie Antoinette's affinity for expensive baubles, court jewellers Charles Böhmer and Paul Bassenge tried to sell her a necklace made from over 500 diamonds that weighed almost 3,000 carats. The queen refused the ostentatious collier, created for Madame du Barry, even after Louis XVI offered to buy it for her as a gift to celebrate the birth of their first child; she told her husband that the money would be better spent on a new warship for France.

In August 1785 she learned someone had bought this costly necklace in her name. A swindler, the Comtesse de la Motte-Valois, pretended to be a close friend of the queen and used forged letters to persuade Cardinal Louis Prince de Rohan, one of France's highest-ranking church officials, that Marie Antoinette was authorizing him to secretly purchase the necklace.

When Rohan wanted to speak with the queen, Madame de la Motte hired a blonde prostitute from the Palais-Royal, named the "Baroness" d'Oliva, coached her to impersonate Marie Antoinette, and arranged a rendezvous with the cardinal. The meeting took place late at night in the Grove of Venus, a secluded wooded area of the Queen's Garden behind the château of Versailles. In the darkness of the park, the cardinal mistakenly believed he had met with the queen, bought the necklace, and gave it to Madame de la Motte. She and her husband promptly sold the diamonds.

On 15 August, Marie Antoinette's official birthday and four days before she was to appear on stage in The Barber of Seville, the king, at her urging, ordered the cardinal arrested in the Hall of Mirrors. This unprecedented scene caused tremendous scandal. The cardinal and Madame de la Motte were sent to the Bastille until tried by the parlement of Paris in the following year.

The cardinal was acquitted, but de la Motte was found guilty and sentenced to life imprisonment. She was also to be publicly stripped, whipped and branded with the letter "V" (for voleuse, thief) in the Cour de Mai of the Palais de Justice.

She struggled so much the bourreau *(executioner) and his assistants could not hold her and, to the crowd's horror, the red-hot branding iron marked her breast rather than her shoulder. After a year in prison, de la Motte escaped to England where she wrote a memoir in which she claimed to be Marie Antoinette's lover.*

Although the queen never met de la Motte and knew nothing about the purchase of the necklace, the French refused to believe she had not been involved. Her reputation for extravagance caused people to believe that she had somehow tricked the cardinal into buying her the necklace. Her reputation was ruined and, for the first time, she was hissed when she attended the theatre. Years later, Napoleon succinctly commented, "The queen's death must be dated from the diamond necklace trial. She was innocent, and, to make sure that her innocence should be publicly known, she chose the parlement *of Paris for her judge. The upshot was that she was universally regarded as guilty."*

The Hôtel de Rohan, the cardinal's lavish home with its famous Salon des Singes *(monkey room) where he entertained Madame de la Motte, is today part of the Archives Nationales in Paris and can be visited [see Other Places, page 151].*

MARIE ANTOINETTE, QUEEN OF FRANCE *(from a portrait by Dufroe, The Metropolitan Museum of Art, Gift of Susan Dwight Bliss, 1956 (56.558.26) Photograph copyright 2006, the Metropolitan Museum of Art).*

The queen was at Trianon running her lines with Madame Campan when the Diamond Necklace Affair broke [See pages 104 and 105]. Despite the magnitude of the scandal, she did not cancel the play and even invited Beaumarchais to attend. He accepted and, in the king's presence, was loudly applauded.

Marie Antoinette, like many of the French, was inspired by the late philosopher Jean Jacques Rousseau (1712–1778), whose writings had become wildly popular. Rousseau stressed the importance of living near nature and the benefits of a tranquil, rural existence. While visiting the Prince of Condé's home at Chantilly [see Other Places, page 156], the queen admired a picturesque *hameau*, or small village, on the estate. In 1783, she selected the far corner of the Petit Trianon's English garden as the site for her own *hameau*.

Marie Antoinette insisted that a working farm be attached to her new *hameau*; the one that she had seen at Chantilly resembled a theatrical set placed in a garden. Richard Mique and painter Hubert Robert began a collaborative effort: an elaborately conceived village and farm resembling those Mique had seen in Normandy. Workers dug an artificial lake, and, using canals, water was pumped in. Mique then constructed a water tower that resembled a lighthouse with a stone base. Called the Marlborough Tower, it was named after a song used in Beaumarchais's *The Marriage of Figaro* that paid tribute to English general John Churchill, first Duke of Marlborough, who fought Louis XIV and was an ancestor of Winston Churchill. The song became so popular that hats, hairstyles and ribbons *à la Marlborough* became the rage throughout France.

Knowing that the queen liked to be surrounded by flowers, Mique ordered 1,732 white and blue glazed flowerpots decorated with her initials from the Saint-Clément ceramic factory, official supplier to the Trianon. He filled the pots with hyacinths and geraniums and used them to cover the *hameau*'s balconies and spiral staircases. One of the

MARIE ANTOINETTE IN HER
"LA BELLE FERMIÈRE" COSTUME.

AXEL, COMTE DE FERSEN.

queen's pages described the profusion of blooms as resembling, "an aerial flowerbed". An abundance of jasmine and roses were planted, and when the summer rain fell, the smell of flowers and freshly cut hay filled the air.

Over the next four years, Mique built a dozen picturesque buildings on the edge of the lake including a mill with a waterwheel used for grinding corn, pigeon loft and a henhouse. The *hameau* had several bungalows for guards and gardeners. These cottages had thatched roofs and, from the outside, resembled shacks. Artists were hired to paint brown or ochre cracks on the outer walls so the little houses appeared weathered. Fissures were added to the plaster, and workmen chipped the brickwork to complete the illusion that time had worn down the exteriors. Gardeners planted honeysuckle and Virginia creeper to climb along the cottages, each of which had its own vegetable garden where cabbages, cauliflowers, and beans were grown. Although the little houses appeared rustic, elegant cabinets, secretaries, and chairs designed by royal furniture makers Reisener and Jacob filled the interiors, and fine tapestries hung on the walls.

Marie Antoinette reserved five buildings for her personal use: the Queen's House, the Billiard House, the boudoir, a mill and a dairy. The Queen's House consisted of two buildings linked by a long open wooden gallery. The house on the right, the Maison de la Reine, held a dining room, gaming room, Chinese cabinet room, and private apartment. The ground floor of the smaller house, the Maison du Billard, was used for billiards, while the upper floor contained a library and sitting room. Food was prepared in the *réchauffoir*, an unpretentious building behind the Queen's House. Although small, this cottage contained several ovens, a stove on which 22 separate pots could cook, and a fireplace with a mechanical spit.

The *hameau* had two dairies. The first was a *laiterie de préparation* where milk was processed into butter or cheese, while these products were served on an elegant porcelain service in the second dairy, the *laiterie de propreté*. This

AXEL FERSEN

On 30 January 1774, 19-year-old Axel, Comte de Fersen (1755–1810), a tall Swedish aristocrat, met a vivacious charmer at a masked ball in Paris. As the evening unfolded, the woman in the black velvet mask chatted with him for a long time before he realized she was the Dauphine. For the next 19 years, Fersen, the same age as Marie Antoinette, proved to be her most faithful friend and possibly her lover. He acted with discretion and never asked for favours. In 1779, when her feelings for him became the subject of conjecture, he left France and travelled to America to serve as aide-de-camp to General Rochambeau during the War of Independence.

In June 1783 Fersen returned to Versailles. He wrote to his sister, "I cannot belong to the one person to whom I wish to belong, the one who really loves me, and so I wish to belong to no one." He never married.

The queen helped Fersen become colonel of the Royal Swedish Regiment in France so he could remain in the country and secretly provided him with a small room on an upper floor of her petits appartements at Versailles. She even had the room redone to accommodate an unusual Swedish stove he requested to be warmer. They exchanged gifts – after the queen admired Fersen's beloved greyhound, he bought her a similar dog.

Marie Antoinette only conceived once when Fersen was in France. This was with her second son, Louis-Charles, born on 27 March 1785, amid conjecture that Fersen fathered this child. The queen adored the cherubic, robust little boy and called him her chou d'amour (sweetheart).

One of Fersen's descendants published edited versions of his correspondence with the queen. One letter, however, written in code, remained as it was originally written. The queen ended this letter, dated 4 July 1791, by calling Fersen the "most loved and most loving of men."

china, decorated with tiny pink flowers and green garlands, came from the queen's own porcelain manufactory located on the Rue Thiroux in Paris. The *laiterie de propreté* was the last building added to the *hameau*. Not only were its floors and walls made from white marble, fifteen marble-topped tables sat inside and were used in making butter, cream and cheese. Although stories that Marie Antoinette pretended to be a shepherdess while at the *hameau* were untrue, she did learn to make butter using beautifully decorated churns.

Mique created a bucolic wonderland for the queen, who soon exchanged late night gambling escapades to rise early in the morning and watch crops being planted. Happy to trade her crown for a straw hat, Marie Antoinette loved to stand on the upper floor of the wooden gallery at the Queen's House and languidly watch the activities of her farm. She often entertained the royal family here and gave dances in a large barn.

Three families lived at the *hameau*: those of the caretaker and gardener, and a farmer with two children who resided on the ten-acre farm just to the north. Marie Antoinette became friendly with these families and often visited to chat while eating the fresh raspberries, strawberries and cherries that were grown here. At the farm, she led her carefully-groomed white lambs to pasture on pretty blue ribbons and doted on her herd of Swiss cows, two of which she named Brunette and Blanchette. The *hameau* housed 68 hens whose eggs were often taken to the Petit Trianon's kitchens. Madame Campan wrote, "The pleasure of wandering through the farmyard buildings of the *hameau*, of seeing the cows milked, and of fishing in the lake enchanted the queen."

Both Marie Antoinette and Louis XVI believed their children should learn about animals, and rabbits, goats, sheep and ducks were kept as pets for them. The queen often took her children fishing in a tiny grey rowboat, creating a scene of familial devotion. Over 2,000 carp and pike swam in the artificial lake, and Marie Antoinette allegedly included funds for 600 pounds of bread to feed these fish in the annual budget.

Since so few received invitations to the *hameau* or Trianon theatre, the queen's activities there remained a mystery. Lewd anecdotes were told about her amusements and, as her life was hidden from public view, no one could defend her or dispel these rumours. To the increasingly agitated Parisians, the private sanctuary she created became a symbol: an evil place where the queen hatched cruel plots against her simple, unsuspecting subjects.

Marie Antoinette seemed unable to comprehend that, while she enjoyed a fantasy world of rustic simplicity, many of her subjects lived in real hovels on the edge of famine. American statesman Gouverneur Morris (1752–1816), who served as minister of the United States in France on the eve of revolution, witnessed this paradox. After visiting the *hameau* in May 1789, he wrote, "Here royalty indulges in massive expenditure to conceal itself from its own eyes, but the attempt is vain. A dairy furnished with the porcelain of Sèvres is a semblance too splendid of rural life … The money applied in making this garden has been badly spent and could be barely spared."

Genuinely confused about how to govern France, the well-intentioned king seemed unable to rule decisively and became increasingly depressed and withdrawn. In a desperate attempt to repair the economy, he agreed to summon the Estates-General, an assembly of elected representatives of the clergy, nobility and commoners (or the Third Estate). The first session was on 5 May 1789 in the Hôtel des Menus Plaisirs at Versailles [see Other Places, pages 156].

Personal tragedies diverted the royal couple's attention from the country's political crisis. The youngest of their four children, Sophie, died in June 1787, aged only 11 months. The queen invited family members to sit with her by the tiny corpse and share her sorrow. She worried continually about the health of her elder son, Dauphin Louis-Joseph, who had suffered for several years with tuberculosis and spent every spare minute with him in his room filled with books and toy soldiers. On 4 June 1789, the eight-year-old died with his mother at his bedside.

The following month, violence erupted in Paris after the king abruptly dismissed Jacques Necker, the popular controller-general of finances. After several days of riots, an armed crowd stormed the prison of the Bastille in the Rue Saint-Antoine. A courtier woke the king on 15 July saying, "The Bastille has been taken. The governor has been killed, and his head is being carried on a pike through the town." Stunned, Louis asked, "Then this is a revolt?" The answer came, "No, Sire, it is a revolution."

Although Marie Antoinette urged her husband to leave Versailles and move further from the bloodthirsty Parisians, the king decided that he and his immediate family should stay. His youngest brother and others in the royal family emigrated for their safety that very night disguised as servants. Almost all the queen's friends, including the Duchesse de Polignac, quickly left the country.

On 5 October 1789 Marie Antoinette, accompanied by a single footman, made a rare visit to the *hameau*. Still despondent over her son's death, she had not seen her country village in months. Although the sky was overcast, she planned to inspect the farm. After giving orders for the coming winter, the queen milked a cow, watered her plants, and afterwards stopped in the grotto by the Petit Trianon to rest. Sitting on a bed of moss, she saw one of her pages running toward her, clearly agitated. He handed her a note. It said an armed mob of angry Parisians was marching to Versailles to demand bread and wanted the royal family to return to the capital with them – the impending attack could occur within an hour. The queen hurriedly walked back to the château through the mist and drizzle. She would never return to her beloved Trianon.

MARIE ANTOINETTE AND LOUIS XVI, TWO ANONYMOUS PORTAITS FROM THE 1780S.

The Metropolitan Museum of Art, Gift of Susan Dwight Bliss, 1956 (56.558.23 and 56.558.24) Photographs copyright 2006, the Metropolitan Museum of Art.

"I have ever believed that had there been no queen, there would have been no revolution." – Thomas Jefferson

ON 5 OCTOBER 1789 RIOTS BROKE OUT IN THE CAPITAL. THE PARISIANS, ALREADY ANGRY THAT BAKERIES HAD NO BREAD, HEARD RUMOURS THAT OFFICERS OF THE ROYAL ARMY HAD TRAMPLED revolutionary tricolour cockades at a banquet held in the Opera House at Versailles. The dinner had been given on 1 October by officers of the royal bodyguards to welcome the Flanders Regiment, which the king had transferred to Versailles to reinforce the palace guard. Louis XVI and Marie Antoinette briefly attended the festivities, and the queen carried the rosy-cheeked new Dauphin, four-year-old Louis-Charles, in her arms. Propaganda pamphlets distributed around the capital depicted the banquet as an anti-revolutionary orgy. Incidentally, Marie Antoinette never said "let them eat cake" and even Louis XVIII, no admirer of his former sister in law, attributed the phrase to Rousseau. Rousseau claimed another princess, Marie-Therese, wife of Louis XIV, made the statement in 1740.

Over 5,000 disgruntled market women gathered in Paris and decided to march 11 miles to Versailles to confront the king and ask for grain or flour. Many demanded that he return with them to the city. Still loyal to Louis XVI, they believed if he lived near them he could solve their problems and not be swayed by his wife or courtiers who were "against the people".

Armed with pikes, axes, clubs, large kitchen knives, pitchforks and old muskets, the women, many of them *poissardes* (fishwives) wearing red dresses and white hats, shouted venomous threats directed at Marie Antoinette.

Voices yelled, "We want the Queen!" Their angry ravings escalated: "I'll hack off her head and take it back to Paris on a pike." " I'll fry the bitch's liver." " I'll open her belly, stick my arm in up to the elbow, and pull out her guts." Madame Campan described these women as "furies, who wore white aprons, which they screamed out were intended to receive the bowels of Marie Antoinette, and that they would make cockades of them, mixing the most obscene expressions with these horrible threats."

Accompanied by 10 drummers, the marchers plodded on through thick fog and driving rain, which quickly turned the road to mud. The procession swelled to around 7,000 as men, including some dressed in female costume, joined the crowd; they knew that the king's troops would not fire on women.

When Marie Antoinette arrived at the château from Trianon, she found the palace in turmoil. Courtiers swarmed through the great reception rooms and paced the Hall of Mirrors asking questions with growing uneasiness. They watched from windows as sentries tried to fasten iron grilles and gates that had not been locked since being installed 100 years earlier. Many rusty hinges only turned with great difficulty.

In anticipation of the crowd's arrival, a division of the king's troops lined up in formation in the Place d'Armes between the *Grande Écurie*, the stables which still stand across from the château, and the main gates. Other guards waited inside the front courtyard with the National Guard of Versailles, who intimated they would not fire on the Parisians.

Messengers hurried to find Louis XVI, who was hunting in the forest at nearby Meudon. At 3.00 pm the king galloped back to the château so alarmed by the news that he rode by the assembled troops without returning their salute. He consulted advisors and the queen. The Comte de Saint-Priest, minister to the King's Household, had prepared for the royal family to leave for the castle at Rambouillet, a greater distance from Paris than Versailles, and to have the château protected by troops loyal to the king. First Louis agreed to go, then, pressured by an official with an opposing view, changed his mind. As counsellors bickered, he wrestled with their suggestions and kept repeating that he did not want to run away or become a "fugitive king". Finally, Louis decided that he and his family would stay although his most experienced military advisors urged him to flee. The Comte de Saint-Priest, antagonizing the king with his fearless polemics, predicted, "Sire, if you allow yourself to be taken to Paris tomorrow, your crown is lost."

The market women began to arrive in Versailles around sunset. Several were selected as representatives and escorted inside to meet the king. Overwhelmed by the château's grandeur, the *parisiennes* humbly asked for bread. The king promised to help, treated them kindly, and even embraced one young girl. The workers' ire had begun to dwindle, when an aide-de-camp of the Marquis de La Fayette, commander of the new National Guard in Paris, arrived with a note from the general. He informed the king that 20,000 troops, whose loyalty was uncertain, had insisted on following the market women to Versailles.

With the eminent arrival of these soldiers, Louis finally agreed to go to Rambouillet with his family. Just before eight, Marie Antoinette ran to her children's rooms and told the staff to prepare to leave in 15 minutes. She was hurriedly packing as the order was sent to the royal stables to prepare for the trip. When the raucous crowd saw the gates of the stables swing open, they roared with anger and stopped the carriages by unharnessing the horses, which they led away.

The king's advisors then offered their own carriages, which waited at a different exit, but the royal couple refused. Ministers begged Marie Antoinette to escape with the children while she could, but she replied, "My place is by the king. I do not wish him to face dangers that I do not share."

The queen knew she was the principal target for the malcontents and gave instructions to royal governess Madame de Tourzel, to take the Dauphin to the king if there was an attack. She told the governess, "I would rather expose myself to any danger that there may be, and draw the crowd away from the king and my children." Impressed with her courage, de Tourzel remembered, "Her countenance was serene … No one could have read in it the slightest sign of alarm. She reassured everyone, thought of everything."

Axel Fersen, along with other friends, sat with Marie Antoinette in the *Salon Doré* of her *petits appartements* during that long night. Although the queen found the Parisians' hatred of her incomprehensible, she remained calm. "I know they are coming for my head," she declared, "but I have learned from my mother not to fear death."

Just after midnight, the venerated La Fayette (1757–1834) arrived at the château with the National Guard of Paris. La Fayette, who had fought in the American War of Independence, was known as a champion of democracy, and the king and queen did not trust him. Exhausted, splattered with mud, the war hero staggered up the palace steps, and dramatically announced to the king, "Sire, I bring my head to save that of Your Majesty." When the king asked him what his troops wanted, La Fayette replied that, just as the Parisians asked for bread, the National Guard wanted the privilege of guarding the king. Louis retorted, "Well then, let them do so." He agreed to replace his personal bodyguard with the antiroyalist National Guard and sent many of his troops to Rambouillet. La Fayette assured the king and queen that he would answer for the troops from Paris and suggested they get some rest. The crowd began to disperse as the market women tried to find warm, dry places to sleep. It seemed as if the crisis had been averted.

Marie Antoinette disliked La Fayette, but she believed, as did the king and many others, that he probably had full control over his troops. When the man whom Madame Campan described as "the idol of Paris" advised them not to worry, the king and queen felt certain they were in safe hands. While La Fayette rode his white charger to the nearby Hôtel de Noailles, his father-in-law's mansion, to sleep, the king dismissed his attendants. Ushers closed the salon doors and extinguished the candles while Marie Antoinette quietly said goodnight to her friends. She went to her formal bedroom at 2.00 am and, exhausted, quickly fell asleep after instructing the ladies of waiting on duty, Madame Auguié, sister to Madame Campan, and Madame Thibault, to go to bed. The women, absolutely devoted to the queen and highly concerned for her safety, decided to hold a vigil outside her bedroom door in the adjoining *Salon des Nobles*.

The Marquis de la Tour du Pin, in charge of the militia, watched the courtyard all night from a window in the Aisle des Ministres, the first building on the left in the château's front courtyard. Around daybreak, he suddenly heard footsteps and saw, to his amazement, a ragged crowd of several hundred brandishing axes and pikes. They swarmed into the front courtyard through a small gate that was usually locked. After shooting the sentinel, the invaders stormed the great marble staircase and pushed their way into the queen's guardroom at the top of the stairs, where only one guard was on duty.

At about the same time, the queen's ladies heard gunshots and screams. Madame Thibault ran to wake up Marie Antoinette while Madame Auguié opened the door of the antechamber leading to the guardroom. She saw the sentry struggling to hold his musket across the door while fighting off the mob. As he turned towards her, she saw that his face was covered in blood. He shouted, "Save the Queen! They have come to assassinate her."

Madame Auguié slammed and bolted the door, ran through the next room (the *Salon des Nobles*) and locked that door as well. Reaching the queen's bedroom, she screamed, "Get out of bed, Madame! Don't stop to dress. Fly to the king's apartment." The women heard fighting, then a scream. The guard was struck on the head and fell as the crowd charged past him shouting, "Death to the Austrian!"

Marie Antoinette quickly slipped a petticoat over her nightgown while Madame Thibault threw a yellow and white striped dressing gown around her shoulders. The women opened a door hidden, then as now, on the left of the huge bed. Covered with the same white silk brocade as the room's wall hangings – a pattern of ribbons and peacock feathers – this concealed door led to the queen's private rooms. The women ran through her private apartments and down a long passage that connected her apartment to that of the king. They reached the hall outside the *Salon de l'Oeil de Boeuf*, adjacent to the king's bedroom. To their surprise, the door, usually unlocked except on the queen's side, was bolted. The three women frantically beat on the door and screamed for help. While they waited, they heard the crowd ransacking her room. Infuriated to find her bed empty, the Parisians shredded the mattress with their pikes.

Finally, a servant came and opened the door into the king's apartment, but Louis was not there. Hearing the commotion, he had run to the queen's bedroom using a secret hallway under the *Salon de l'Oeil de Boeuf*. He found her bed empty and dashed back to his chamber. Madame de Tourzel had just arrived with Louis-Charles, still half-asleep. Marie Antoinette hurried to fetch her daughter, and soon the entire family, including the king's 25-year-old sister Elisabeth, huddled together in the king's bedroom. The invaders, who had slaughtered and beheaded two guards, pushed closer until the family could hear axe blows on the panels of the doors of the *Oeil de Boeuf*. Suddenly the noise stopped, and they heard approaching footsteps. La Fayette's troops had arrived to clear the château and push the crowd into the front courtyard.

The queen, seated by one of the tall windows in her husband's bedroom, stared down into the *Cour de Marbre*. There were so many people that she couldn't see the stones of the courtyard. She wrapped her arms around her son and daughter, and the sleepy little boy, too young to understand what was happening, kept repeating, "I'm hungry, Mama! I'm so hungry." She hugged the child and gently asked him to be patient and wait for breakfast. On the advice of ministers, the king and his family then appeared onto the low balcony of his bedroom, which overlooked the courtyard, to try and calm the people, who howled, "To Paris... The king to Paris!"

The royal family had stepped back in the king's bedroom when menacing voices in the crowd shouted, "The queen on the balcony." Hearing those ominous words, Marie Antoinette paled. Soon the mob was screaming for *La Reine* and stomping their feet. La Fayette turned to her, gestured to the balcony, and said, "The people are calling for you, Madame. You must show yourself in order to calm them. It is necessary." Amid protests from her family, the queen turned to La Fayette and coolly said, "In that case, I will do it even if it costs me my life."

As she walked toward the balcony, her children ran up to her. She took them by the hand and led them through the glass doors onto the balcony. The crowd shouted in anger, "No children!" Marie Antoinette gently handed the little boy and girl to their governess and stepped forward. As the autumn breeze brushed against her, she stared down at the sea of angry faces, knowing how bitterly they hated her. She confronted the crowd and waited. She could see muskets aimed at her, but did not flinch. The queen stood alone in her white and yellow striped gown for several minutes while her blonde hair, unpowdered and dishevelled, blew around her face like a halo. Finally, she sank into a low curtsey, with her hands crossed on her chest.

Marie Antoinette's courage and natural majesty astounded the crowd. Their wrath melted. La Fayette appeared on the balcony, bowed before the queen, and kissed her hand to show his loyalty. A voice shouted *Vive la Reine!* The crowd echoed, *Vive la Reine!* They continued cheering as the general escorted her back into the king's bedroom. Drained, she picked up her little boy and kissed him feverishly, then collapsed into a chair and wept.

The queen's fearlessness had salvaged some dignity for the royal family, but the crowd began to chant, "To Paris... The king must go to Paris." Louis XVI, without consulting anyone, trudged onto the balcony and announced, "You wish, my children, that I should follow you to Paris: I consent, but on condition that I shall not be separated from my wife and family." Cries of *Vive le Roi!* and *Vive la Nation!* filled the air.

LOUIS XVI AND HIS FAMILY DURING THE ATTACK ON VERSAILLES. A PAINTING BY JULIUS BENCZUR.

Collection of the author.

The royal family left the château using a little staircase, still in existence, which exited into the *Cour de Marbre*. No one wanted them to walk down the main staircase, which was still stained with blood. As Louis XVI stepped into his carriage, he sighed to the Marquis de la Tour du Pin, "You are in charge here. Try to save my poor Versailles for me." Marie Antoinette's daughter wrote in her journal, "We left Versailles at noon. Little did we know that we would never see it again ... the heads of two of our guards, on pikes, led the procession. They still had on their powdered wigs and hats."

The royal family set off for the capital in a procession of 2,000 carriages containing courtiers, ministers and members of the National Assembly, the new name for the Third Estate. The bedraggled mob danced alongside the carriages all the way to Paris arm in arm with soldiers who waved bayonets with loaves of bread stuck on the end. Drunken women straddled cannon and jeered, "They'll give us bread now that we have the baker, the baker's wife, and the little baker's boy". As they approached the city, the festive crowd decided that the still-bleeding heads of the murdered guards should be groomed. They stopped in the town of Sèvres and forced a hairdresser to curl and powder the hair. Fersen rode in a carriage towards the back of the procession. A callused soldier accustomed to the carnage of battle, the Swede described the surreal journey to his father, "I returned to Paris in one of the coaches which followed the king's. We were on the road for six and a half hours [the trip usually took two hours]. God preserve me from ever seeing another spectacle as distressing..."

Just before the Queen left Versailles, Madame Campan spoke with her in her *petits appartements*. In tears, Marie Antoinette was distributing a few mementos to her ladies. She had packed only her diamonds, which she carried in a small jewel case. She hugged Campan, asked her to join them in the capital, and remarked, with a chilling prescience, "When kings become prisoners, they have not long to live."

HOW TO USE THIS BOOK TO TOUR VERSAILLES

The main tour of the State Apartments shows the queen's State Rooms in the opposite order from which they were intended to be seen, ie with the most private room, her bedroom, entered first. To understand how a visitor to the Queen's Apartments during the eighteenth century would have been received, go to the last room of the Queen's Apartments, the Guardroom (just before the Coronation Room). On 6 October 1789 the crowd attacked the sentry in this room as the queen slept in her bedchamber.

Next comes the Antechamber of the Grand Couvert. *Although the king and queen ate in the* Grand Couvert *in public, this room was used more often as a waiting area for those about to see Marie Antoinette. Madame Vigée Lebrun's first painting from life of the queen (1779) wearing court dress usually hangs here, as does her portrait of Marie Antoinette with her three children which was shown in the Salon of 1787 at the Louvre. Two years later, after the death of her older son, the grieving queen asked that this painting, which she usually saw while walking to the chapel, be moved. This probably saved the work from destruction during the château's invasion in 1789.*

Marie Antoinette's ladies sat in the next room, the Salon des Nobles, *the night before the rioters broke into the château. It is next to the queen's bedchamber, most private of her rooms. Here she dressed in public each morning (the* lever) *and prepared for bed each evening (the* coucher). *Marie Antoinette gave birth here four times; the first time was in front of the court and public.*

The wall hangings in the queen's bedroom are exact replicas of the summer silks that hung here in the autumn of 1789. The quilt of the enormous canopied bed is original.

There are actually two concealed doors in the queen's bedroom – one on either side of the bed. Both lead to her private apartments. The door to the left of the bed was used by Marie Antoinette to flee from the crowd. Beside this door sits the queen's massive mahogany jewellery cabinet, made in 1787.

The queen added several personal touches to this stateroom. Portraits of her mother, Empress Maria Theresa, older brother, Emperor Joseph II, and her husband were placed above the three mirrors. In 1770 the corners of the room were redone for Marie Antoinette with the double-headed Austrian eagle alternating with the arms of France and Navarre.

The balcony on which Marie Antoinette faced the crowd in October 1789 can best be seen from the Cour de Marbre, the château's front courtyard. Part of the king's bedchamber, the balcony runs along the centre of the palace. It has an iron and gold grille and is entered by glass doors leading from the bedchamber, which can be seen as part of "the king's apartment" tour.

The château de Versailles is open every day, except Monday, from November through March from 9.00 am to 4.30 pm (last admission at 4.00 pm). From April through October, the château is open from 9.00 am to 5.30 pm (last admission at 5.00 pm). Trains from Paris depart from the Gare Saint-Lazare to the Versailles Rive Droite stop or the RER suburban rail C line ("Vick" train) to Versailles/Rive Gauche station. A guided tour, which leaves from Entrance D, is given of the Opera and Chapel. For information on tours see www.chateauversailles.fr or call 03 1 30 83 76 20 or 03 01 30 83 78 00.

The Petit Trianon is open every day, except on French public holidays. From 26 March to 31 October, it can be toured from noon to 6.30 pm (last admission: 6.00 pm); from 1 November to 25 March, open from noon to 5.30 pm (last admission: 5.00 pm). Note that the Petit Trianon is open on Mondays, when the main château is closed.

THE TOWER OF THE TEMPLE BECAME HOME TO THE ROYAL FAMILY WHEN LOUIS WAS DEPOSED IN 1792.

Collection of the author.

LAST DAY IN PARIS

This walk follows the route of Marie Antoinette as she travelled by tumbril from the Conciergerie to the guillotine in the Place de la Révolution (now the Place de la Concorde) on 16 October 1793. Her body was carted to the cemetery of the Madeleine (now the Chapelle Expiatoire) where the walk ends.

AFTER LEAVING VERSAILLES, THE ROYAL FAMILY WAS FORCED TO LIVE AS UNOFFICIAL PRISONERS AT THE TUILERIES PALACE (BURNED IN 1870) NEAR THE LOUVRE. FOLLOWING AN ABORTIVE ESCAPE masterminded by Axel Fersen in June 1791, they were recaptured near the border of the Austrian Netherlands (modern Belgium) and returned to the capital. Marie Antoinette's brother, Emperor Leopold II of Austria, died the following year, and she did not know the new ruler, her nephew Francis II, who cared little about helping the French royal family. France had gone to war with Austria and Prussia in April 1792, and the queen was suspected of plotting with the enemy.

In early August 1792, revolutionary forces and angry Parisians planned an assault on the Tuileries. The royal family knew of the impending attack and, on 5 August, Gouverneur Morris wryly described their situation as, "Nothing remarkable, only that they were up all night expecting to be murdered." Five days later, the Tuileries was stormed. While Louis XVI, Marie Antoinette and their children sought refuge in the National Assembly, which met in a nearby former riding school, hundreds of loyal Swiss Guards were massacred. The 22-year-old Napoleon Bonaparte was among those who watched as the Parisians mutilated the fallen soldiers. Years later, he said, "The sight of the dead Swiss Guards gave me an idea of the meaning of death such as I have never had since on any of my battlefields. … I saw well-dressed women committing acts of the grossest indecency on the corpses."

The king was deposed, and a new government, the National Convention, sent the royal family to a forbidding medieval tower that had been part of a royal home, the Temple [demolished in the nineteenth century, for its site see Other Places, page 158]. The government arrested their friends and servants, including the delicate Princesse de Lamballe who had returned from safety in England to support the queen. The princess was dragged out of prison and murdered during the September Massacres, when gangs broke into jails and killed 1,300 prisoners, most of whom were innocent. A mob paraded her head, still bearing its long strawberry-blonde curls, on a pike to the Temple, where they planned to make Marie Antoinette kiss the remains of her alleged lover.

Six months later, Louis was tried for treason. He was guillotined on 21 January 1793, in Place de la Révolution (now Place de la Concorde). To royalists, little Louis-Charles now became Louis XVII. Fearing monarchist plots to kidnap him, jailors took the child from his mother and kept him on a separate floor of the tower. Shattered, Marie Antoinette waited for hours each day at a window hoping to see a glimpse of her son.

Officers woke the former queen in the middle of the night on 2 August to transfer her to the Conciergerie prison for trial by the Revolutionary Tribunal. She was not allowed to say goodbye to Louis-Charles, but bid a quick emotional farewell to her sister-in-law and daughter, who recalled, "My mother had to stop at the bottom of the tower while municipals drew up papers for her discharge. As she went out, she knocked her head on the last beam, which was lower than she thought. One of the men asked if she had hurt herself. 'No," she replied, "nothing can hurt me now."

STOP ONE: LA CONCIERGERIE

U SED AS A ROYAL RESIDENCE FROM THE TENTH TO THE FOURTEENTH CENTURY, THE CONCIERGERIE, WAS PART OF A COMPLEX OF BUILDINGS THAT HOUSED THE REVOLUTIONARY TRIBUNAL AND VARIOUS courts of law. Considered one of Paris's worst prisons, it was used for temporary confinement for those awaiting trial and called, "the antechamber to the scaffold," as few who entered ever left except to face the executioner. Built next to the Seine, it stayed so damp that water trickled down the walls. The prison was overrun with rats, had no latrines or running water, and the stench was almost unbearable.

Around 3.00 am, Marie Antoinette, now called the "widow Capet", a reference to one of her husband's ancestral names, was led into the jail and signed in as prisoner number 280. The concierge's wife, Marie-Anne Richard, and her young maid, Rosalie Lamorlière, had waited up to greet the former queen. Dressed in a tattered black gown, she carried her little dog along with a bundle containing some clothes, a handkerchief and a bottle of smelling salts.

When the women showed Marie Antoinette the dark stone cell, she seemed stunned. Although in custody for several years, she had never seen a prison for criminals. She glanced around at the bare furnishings: an iron bed with straw mattress, small table, two chairs with cane bottoms, china pitcher and a pail. Her cell, formerly used as a council chamber, had been divided in two by a wooden partition and screen that partially shielded her from two guards who would now watch her day and night. Old peeling wallpaper decorated with fading fleur-de-lis, a symbol of French royalty, was the only decoration. Exhausted and perspiring from the intense August heat, Marie

VISITING THE CONCIERGERIE

  Marie Antoinette's cell, as shown today, is a recreation of the first cell in which she stayed. During the Bourbon Restauration, Louis XVIII ordered that the former queen's second cell be made into a commemorative chapel, which can be toured. Her bed lay at the chapel's entrance; only the floor remains from her original cell. Both cells in which she stayed looked out onto the women's courtyard, which remains much the same as in the 1790s and still has the fountain where female prisoners washed their clothes and one of the stone tables at which they could eat.

Antoinette thanked the women, hung her little gold watch, a childhood gift from her mother, on a nail high on the wall and sank onto the bed.

The next few weeks passed in a monotonous blur. Forbidden to knit or do needlework, she managed to pick out some threads from an old piece of fabric and amused herself by weaving them together. She played with her pug and, although she had never enjoyed reading, pored over the few books she was given: *The Journals of Captain Cook*, a tale that had captivated her husband, *A Voyage to Venice* and *The History of Famous Sea Wrecks*. She sat for hours watching the guards play cards and waiting for her meals. She ate well, usually chicken with vegetables and bouillon. The market women, who hated her when she was queen, now pitied her and saved their best peaches and melons for her. They handed the fruit to Madame Richard, asked her to give them to Marie Antoinette, and refused payment.

Although not allowed to leave her cell, she rose every morning at dawn when guards with fierce mastiffs opened the cells to allow other prisoners to walk in the courtyards. Her cell had one barred ground-level window facing the *Cour des Femmes*, where female prisoners gathered to talk and wash their clothes in a fountain that still exists.

One day Madame Richard brought her eight-year-old son to visit the former queen. Marie Antoinette burst into tears when she saw the child and confided to the concierge's wife how much she missed her own children. Denied the right to send or receive letters, Marie Antoinette was completely cut off from family and friends. Although Fersen, then in Brussels, desperately plotted to save her, she did not know it. He wrote to his sister, Sophie, "My greatest happiness would be to die for her. I begrudge myself the very air I breathe when I think she is locked up in that horrible prison."

As queen, she had often inspired devotion in her servants and now found an unlikely ally in 24-year-old Rosalie, who burned dried shrubs and juniper in her cell to mask foul odours. The maid lent her a cardboard box and

MARIE ANTOINETTE IN HER CELL AT THE CONCIERGERIE. A PAINTING BY CHARLES LOUIS MULLER.

Collection of the author.

remembered that Marie Antoinette was as delighted "as if it had been the most beautiful piece of furniture in the world." She carefully stored her dresses, caps, handkerchiefs, and underwear in it. A few weeks later Rosalie gave her a small red hand mirror with painted Chinese figures that she had purchased in a stall by the Seine. Touched at the young woman's generosity, Marie Antoinette, who still believed that her family in Austria would secure her freedom, told Rosalie that if she were allowed to leave prison, she would take her as her maid.

Visiting the Conciergerie to see the former queen became a tourist attraction. Visitors bribed prison officials to let them peer inside her cell, and this lucrative side business made it easy for the Marquis de Rougeville, a former royal officer, to approach her with an escape plan. In early September, he paid his way into her cell and threw a bouquet of red carnations at her feet. Inside was hidden a note detailing preparations to free her. As she had no pen or pencil, Marie Antoinette answered by pricking words on a scrap of paper with a pin. She handed her reply to a guard she trusted and asked him to give it to the visitor upon his return. The guard betrayed her to authorities. The kindly prison concierge and his wife were imprisoned, and the former queen was interrogated about the "Carnation Conspiracy", then moved to a more secure cell.

Dark and almost entirely underground, Marie Antoinette's second cell was described as the "most damp, unhealthy, fetid, and horrible in Paris". Previously used as a pharmacy, it smelled strongly of medicine. There was no stove or heat, and the cell was bitterly cold. When she requested another blanket, public prosecutor Fouquier-Tinville threatened the concierge with execution for asking favours for the former queen. The harsh conditions affected Marie Antoinette's health; she became sick and began to haemorrhage.

France had declared war against Austria and Prussia, and anti-Austrian sentiment swelled. Petitions demanding the trial of the "Austrian she-wolf" flooded the Convention. Although Jacques Hébert, editor of the influential radical newspaper *Le Père Duchesne,* insisted the former queen's execution was necessary to continue the Revolution's momentum, others felt there was not enough evidence to convict her. In a meeting of the powerful Committee of Public Safety, Hébert bellowed, "I have promised [my readers] the head of Antoinette. I will go and cut if off myself if there is any delay in giving it to me."

Soon an allegation from Marie Antoinette's eight-year-old son gave the revolutionaries the final piece of evidence they felt they needed. After being plied with alcohol, Louis-Charles signed a confession that his mother and aunt had taught him to masturbate and had engaged in incest with him. Members of the Revolutionary Tribunal interrogated the queen's daughter and sister-in-law regarding the boy's statements. Fifteen-year-old Marie-Thérèse wrote that, during her three-hour examination, "in spite of my tears, they pressed me to answer things which I did not understand, but what I understood was so horrible that I cried with indignation."

On 5 October Fouquier-Tinville wrote to the President of the Convention that the "widow Capet" should be immediately tried. She first appeared before the Revolutionary Tribunal in a preliminary hearing at 6.00 pm on 12 October. The Conciergerie was located almost directly under the Grande Chambre where the Revolutionary Tribunal met. This upper floor of the Palais de Justice had formerly been used by the old *parlement* of Paris.

The 37-year-old *ci-devant* queen, in her mended black dress and a white muslin shawl, was accused of conspiring with France's enemies and sending vast sums of money to the Austrian emperor. She was appointed two lawyers, who, although honest and skilled, were given less than two days to review documents and prepare her defence. One of them was noted lawyer Claude Chauveau-Lagarde, who had recently represented Charlotte Corday, a young zealot who murdered Revolutionary leader Jean-Paul Marat. The lawyers helped Marie Antoinette write a letter asking that the trial be delayed so they could familiarize themselves with the case, but her request was never answered.

The trial of the former queen, one of the most anticipated and sensational events of the Revolution, began on 15 October. There were 12 carefully selected jurors. A large crowd packed behind the balustrades of the rectangular courtroom, now the First Chamber of the Civil Court (*Première Chambre Civile*), to watch the proceedings with undivided attention. A group of women, the *tricoteuses* who frequented trials and executions, sat knitting as the prisoner was brought in.

Marie Antoinette, seated in an armchair on a raised platform, listened carefully as 41 witnesses, including hairdressers, servants from Versailles, politicians, soldiers and a shopkeeper testified against her. Most testimony was hearsay or based on missing documents, and only one or two witnesses had actually met Marie Antoinette. When those who knew the prisoner referred to her as "the queen" or "Her Majesty", the prosecutor angrily interrupted them. During cross-examination, Marie Antoinette answered courageously and concisely. Many questions pertained to her correspondence with Austrian relatives, but she was also asked about Jeanne Lamotte, the Diamond Necklace Affair, and her expenditures, including costs at the Petit Trianon.

The prosecutor's most explosive charge was the only one that received no immediate reply from Marie Antoinette. After hearing herself accused of incest with Louis-Charles, she winced and looked away. The interrogation turned along other lines when a juror stood and asked, "Would you kindly observe to the accused that she has not replied… regarding what happened between herself and her son?"

Dead silence fell over the courtroom. Marie Antoinette stood and, with a tremor in her voice, said, "If I have not answered, it was because nature recoils from such an accusation against a mother." She turned to the spectators, and continued, "I appeal to all mothers who may be here!" A murmur of respect rippled through the crowd, and the *tricoteuses* grew so unruly that the session had to be stopped for several minutes.

The first day's proceedings lasted 15 hours, and the second day ran an hour longer. As the trial closed, the prosecutor asked if Marie Antoinette had anything to say that might add to her defence. She stood and defiantly stated, "Yesterday I did not know the witnesses, and I was ignorant of what they would testify. Well, no one has said anything definitively against me. I end by declaring that I was only Louis XVI's wife, and that I was bound to submit to his will."

The prosecutor delivered his closing argument, followed by Chauveau-Lagarde. Marie Antoinette was led to a small room next to the Grand Chamber, where she waited for the verdict. Around 4.00 am on 16 October she listened as she was found guilty on all counts. The prosecutor asked for, and received, the sentence of death. Public execution would take place within a few hours. Offered a chance to speak, she calmly shook her head. As she was led out of the courtroom by torchlight, the jurors congratulated each other. One of them, Trinchard, wrote to his brother, "I'd like to tell you that I was one of the jury who judged that ferocious beast who has devoured most of the Republic, that woman who they used to call the Queen of France."

Marie Antoinette returned to her cell and asked for a pen and paper. By the flickering light of two small candles, she wrote an extraordinary last letter to Elisabeth, her sister-in-law who was still imprisoned in the Temple: "I have just been sentenced, not to a shameful death, that is only for criminals, but to join your brother. Innocent like him... I am calm as one is when one's conscience is clear. I deeply regret having to abandon my poor children." She brought up her son's allegations of sexual abuse: "I know how much my little boy must have made you suffer. Forgive him, remember how young he is, and how easy it is to make a child say whatever one wants, to put words he does not understand into his mouth." She bid farewell to her family, and added, "I had friends. The thought of being separated from them forever and of their distress is among my greatest regrets in dying. Let them know that down to the last moments, they were in my mind." She ended by writing, "I kiss you with my entire heart, as well as my poor dear children. My God! How agonizing it is to leave them forever. … Adieu, may this letter reach you."

She finished as the sun came up. When Rosalie entered, she found Marie Antoinette lying on her bed crying. Rosalie offered some broth, and she ate a few mouthfuls. Around 8.00 am, the maid helped her dress. Guards stood and watched the former queen change clothes, though she begged for privacy. She slipped on a white piqué gown and the last remaining souvenir of her former life: elegant plum-coloured slippers with pointed toes and a curved dainty heel. She covered her shoulders with a linen shawl and put on a small bonnet. When the young executioner Charles Henri Sanson arrived, she was on her knees praying. Tall and muscular, Sanson was the son of the famous executioner who beheaded the former Louis XVI, and several generations of the family had served as public executioners. He was dressed in the traditional uniform of striped trousers, dark green coat, and tri-cornered hat.

Marie Antoinette protested when told she would be bound, but Sanson brutally pulled her arms behind her back and tied her hands. He took off her bonnet, set her on a wooden stool, and, using a large pair of scissors, cropped her hair so that it would not interfere with the guillotine's blade. When Marie Antoinette looked away, he stuffed her hair into his pocket; by tradition, hair of the condemned, often sold to wig-makers, became the executioner's property.

Leaving the Conciergerie, turn right onto Boulevard du Palais. The Cour du Mai is the courtyard in front of the Palace of Justice; look for its ornate iron grill.

MARIE ANTOINETTE BROUGHT TO THE GUILLOTINE (AFTER A DRAWING BY JACQUES-LOUIS DAVID WHO WITNESSED THE EXECUTION) ALONG WITH A NINETEENTH-CENTURY ILLUSTRATION.

Private collection.

STOP TWO: THE COUR DU MAI OF THE PALAIS DE JUSTICE

4, BOULEVARD DU PALAIS

Métro: Cité

At 11:00 AM MOUNTED POLICE AND FOOT SOLDIERS LINED UP BY THE GIANT STAIRCASE IN THE FRONT COURTYARD OF THE PALACE OF JUSTICE. SURROUNDED BY GUARDS, MARIE ANTOINETTE walked through the prison door and into the bright daylight. At the top of a short flight of steps, a wooden cart, a tumbril, used to transport criminals, waited to take her to the guillotine in the Place de la Révolution. Her husband had gone to his execution in a closed carriage as a safety precaution, and she expected to be transported the same way. When she saw the open two-wheeled cart with its single white horse, her self-assurance crumbled. Trembling, Marie Antoinette told the guards that she did not believe she would arrive at the guillotine but would be bludgeoned to death in the street.

An enormous crowd waited outside the ornate wrought-iron railings of the *Cour du Mai*, the courtyard in front of the Palace of Justice. They watched as Marie Antoinette climbed into the tumbril and automatically turned to ride facing the horse. Sanson stopped her and made her sit with her back to the horse so that she could not avoid the crowd. She gingerly lowered herself on the narrow plank. The executioner stood behind her holding one end of the rope that bound her hands, which he showed to the crowd.

Mounted soldiers and gendarmes surrounded the cart, and the gates were then swung open. As the procession began, there were cries of "There she is! There she is!" Marie Antoinette braced her feet in the hope of being able to keep her balance as the cart moved off and began to bounce over the cobblestones.

OFF WITH THEIR HEADS

On 10 October 1789, Parisian doctor, Joseph-Ignace Guillotin, proposed to the National Assembly that execution by decapitation, with no torture preceding, should become the sole capital punishment in France. Guillotin, also a member of the National Assembly, suggested that all those committing crimes should be punished in the same way. Until the 1790s, the wealthy tended to be killed with a sword or axe, while commoners were burned at the stake, broken on the wheel, or drawn-and-quartered. France adopted the guillotine as its sole method of capital punishment in 1791 although executioners bitterly opposed its introduction. They complained that the guillotine's efficiency robbed their profession of its drama and insisted that merely pulling a lever to release a blade demeaned their skills.

The guillotine did not always ensure quick death; if the blade had become dull, several chops were needed. Originally, the machine had been designed with a curved blade, and, allegedly, Louis XVI reviewed the design and suggested a triangular one. Dr Guillotin tried his machine out on sheep and corpses to perfect it, and there was a great deal of speculation about whether a separated head would continue to think or speak. Wild stories abounded about severed heads with lips moving, eyes winking. Some clamed that they had seen severed heads responding to their name being called. The guillotine found its way into French culture.

In Paris, the guillotine operated in several locations including the former Place Louis XV, renamed Place de la Révolution (now Place de la Concorde). When neighbouring shops complained about the smell and blood, it was moved to the Barrière du Trône (now Place de la Nation). Initially intrigued by the efficient machine, which severed head in less than a second, the Parisians flocked to watch as thousands climbed the scaffold. The guillotine was the only method of execution used in France until the death penalty was abolished in 1981.

Walk back along Boulevard du Palais toward the Conciergerie, and cross the Seine on the Pont au Change. Turn left onto Quai de la Mégisserie. Follow along the river and turn right onto Rue du Pont Neuf. Turn left onto Rue Saint-Honoré. Continue past Rue du Louvre, The Temple de l'Oratoire will be on your left just past Rue de l'Oratoire. Proceed down Rue Saint-Honoré to the site of Rose Bertin's boutique, which was on the left side of the street where the antique gallery of Le Louvre des Antiquaires is now located (2, Place du Palais-Royal). The Palais-Royal will be a block further on your right [see Other Places, page 150]. Continue past Rue des Pyramides, and past the Church of Saint-Roch at 296, Rue Saint-Honoré.

THE THÉÂTRE FRANÇAIS ON RUE SAINT-HONORÉ.

SEVERAL HOURS EARLIER, PARIS HAD AWAKENED TO THE STEADY BEAT OF DRUMS. CROWDS HURRIED THROUGH THE RIGHT BANK EAGER TO FIND A SPOT WITH A GOOD VIEW. TRAFFIC THROUGHOUT THE heart of the city had been suspended, and 30,000 armed troops now lined the streets. Cannon had been placed on every bridge and intersection between the jail and guillotine, as officials feared that royalists or Marie Antoinette's relatives would attempt to stage a rescue. Spectators gathered in every window overlooking the route, and those who lived in nearby buildings invited friends to watch with them or rented their roofs and balconies to those eager to see the proceedings.

An eyewitness wrote, "I heard a mother say to her daughter, 'above all, don't cry when you see her; you will get us guillotined!'" and described the tumbril as looking, "like a dung cart; when it bumped over the cobbles, you could hear it crack as though it would break." As the escort accompanying the procession shouted, "Make way for the Austrian woman," the tumbril crossed the Pont au Change and the Place du Châtelet. It turned left onto the narrow Rue Saint-Honoré, then the main east-west thoroughfare of the Right Bank.

Marie Antoinette sat proudly in the cart, holding her head high and looking straight ahead. At the corner of the Rue du Roule, near the Pont-Neuf, she noticed tricolour flags and stared at them. From time to time, she read signs in front of shops. She knew the Rue Saint-Honoré well; her coach had sped along the winding street countless times on the way to the Opera or the Tuileries. As the cart rolled westward, the Parisians stared in silence at the prisoner.

A CONTEMPORARY IMAGE OF MARIE ANTOINETTE'S EXECUTION ON 16 OCTOBER 1793.

akg-images

They were astonished at her appearance. The free-spirited elegant queen had become a gaunt old woman with white hair, hollow cheeks, and shadows that encircled her eyes.

At the Temple de l'Oratoire, a mother held her child up in the air. When he blew a kiss to Marie Antoinette, her composure faltered, but she quickly regained control of her emotions. Soon the procession neared the former shop of Rose Bertin at 149, Rue Saint-Honoré by the Place du Palais-Royal and passed beneath the balcony where Bertin and her seamstresses had curtseyed to the queen as she rode by in her carriage years before.

The cart slowed at the Palais-Royal, home of her husband's cousin and outspoken enemy, Philippe Egalité, the former Duc d'Orleans. Marie Antoinette knew he was now held in the Conciergerie. The anti-royalist activity he had allowed at the *palais* caused it to be known as "the home of the Revolution". Then as now, galleries filled with shops and cafes sat behind the palace, Outside one of these cafes, on 12 July 1789, writer Camille Desmoulins had leapt onto a table and incited the Parisians to storm the Bastille [see Other Places, page 153].

As the tumbril reached the Church of Saint-Roch, insults suddenly rained down on Marie Antoinette; a woman standing on the church steps spat at her. An actor named Grammont appeared on a horse waving a sword and joking. He yelled, "Here she is, my friends, the infamous Antoinette. Look at the tigress now!". He cursed the crowd for not being more hostile and tried to goad them into attacking her. She gave no sign of panic, and stared straight ahead.

Standing on a balcony on the north side of the street and chatting with a politician's wife, Jacques-Louis David waited for the procession. He held an artist's pad and pencils. As the cart approached, he looked down and quickly sketched Marie Antoinette in profile. This drawing, now in the Louvre, became one of David's most famous works.

As the tumbril approached the Rue Royale, a woman in a window yelled, "Death to the *Autrichienne*!". Marie Antoinette glanced up at her. Her eyes blazed as she recognized one of her former waiting women from Versailles.

STOP FOUR: PLACE DE LA RÉVOLUTION

(NOW THE PLACE DE LA CONCORDE)

Métro: Concorde

AN HOUR AFTER LEAVING THE CONCIERGERIE, THE PROCESSION ROUNDED THE CORNER OF THE RUE ROYALE AND APPROACHED THE PLACE DE LA RÉVOLUTION. SPECTATORS POURED INTO THE SQUARE and, eager not to miss anything, ran back and forth, asking each other, "Should I watch from the head side or body side?" Some even climbed the large equestrian statues for a better view. Many parents had brought children and held them on their shoulders. Vendors hawked sticky buns, fruit and drinks to the waiting crowd. Some sold guillotine souvenirs such as special programmes of the day's events.

The tumbril then passed the Hôtel du Garde Meuble, the royal furniture warehouse, and its sister mansion [see Other Places, page 152], and pulled into the large open square. The cart slowly approached the tall platform that held the 15-foot-high guillotine, located approximately where the obelisk sits today. Large contingents of armed gendarmes stood around the scaffold. Behind them pressed a sea of people; men, women, and young children who waited to see how the former queen would react in the face of death – whether she would beg for her life or bravely face execution.

When Marie Antoinette saw the Tuileries, where she had been so joyfully welcomed on her first trip to Paris as Dauphine, her face turned red. Newspaper reports stated that her eyes filled with tears. Sanson helped her out of the cart. She stood motionless and looked up to cast her first and only glance at the guillotine. The polished triangular blade glittered brightly in the sun. Some accounts relate that a priest loyal to the Revolution who accompanied her whispered, "This is the moment, Madame, to arm yourself with courage." She replied, "Courage! I've shown it for years; do you think I will lose my courage now when my sufferings are about to end?"

Although her hands were tied, she nimbly climbed the steep wooden stairs to the platform and quickly walked to the guillotine. As Sanson bound her onto a wooden plank, she lost one of her shoes and accidentally stepped on his foot. She whispered an apology as the neck collar slid around her. A drum-roll began as the plank was pushed forward. For a long moment, she lay face down with the back of her neck exposed underneath the blade. She could see the dark red wicker basket filled with sawdust waiting to receive her severed head. The blade fell at 12.15. The crowd roared as the executioner reached into the basket, seized her head by its thin, white hair and strode around the platform displaying it.

Leave the Place de la Concorde by the northwestern exit (by the Hôtel Crillon at 10, Place de la Concorde). Turn right onto Rue Boissy d'Anglas. Turn left onto Rue du Faubourg Saint-Honoré. Turn right onto the narrow Rue d'Anjou. Cross Rue de Surène and Rue Lavoisier (named after noted chemist Antoine-Laurent Lavoisier, guillotined in 1794). The Place Louis XVI and the Chapelle Expiatoire will be on your right.

OVERJOYED, THE CROWD SHOUTED *"VIVE LA RÉPUBLIQUE!"* AS THE EXECUTIONER'S ASSISTANT UNBOUND HER BLEEDING BODY FROM THE PLANK AND TOSSED IT INTO A LARGE BASKET. SANSON threw her head in after it, and her remains were carted to the nearby cemetery of the Madeleine, which served as resting place for those put to death on the Place de la Révolution.

Rather than being buried in a common trench, she was to be placed in a special ditch, like that in which her husband had been buried. The body reached the cemetery around 1.00 pm when the gravedigger, Joly, and his assistants were taking their midday break. A young wax modeller, the demure Marie Grosholtz (who later became famous as Madame Tussaud) had secretly been instructed by the National Convention to go to the cemetery and make a death mask of the former queen.

The men who unloaded the cart saw no officials and, eager to get to lunch, flung Marie Antoinette's body on the grass and put her head between her legs. Grosholtz crept up and gently lifted the head. She put it in her lap, opened her bag, and pulled out wax and tools.

Grosholtz had known the royal family and lived at Versailles teaching Marie Antoinette's sister-in-law, Elisabeth to make wax models of birds and flowers. The queen sometimes stopped by to watch the lessons. Although she often made death masks and was inured to the macabre craft, Grosholtz wrote that the sight of Marie Antoinette's staring eyes haunted her the rest of her life. Thirty minutes later, she quietly left with the finished death mask in her bag.

The former queen's body lay on the ground for several days before she was buried near her husband. Eventually, Madame Elisabeth, Philippe Egalité, Madame du Barry, and almost 3,000 others who had been guillotined were brought to this cemetery, then in an unpopulated area surrounded by cornfields. The cemetery became full in 1794 and was closed. A royalist bought the land and planted weeping willow trees above the royal graves.

After the downfall of Napoleon's regime in 1814, Marie Antoinette's brother-in-law, the former Comte de Provence, returned to France as Louis XVIII. He ordered the bodies of Marie Antoinette and Louis XVI to be exhumed. On the twenty-second anniversary of Louis XVI's execution, a grand procession carried the coffins to the crypt of the Saint-Denis basilica [see Other Places, page 155], the traditional necropolis for Bourbon monarchs.

Two years later, Louis XVIII commissioned architect Pierre Fontaine to build the Chapelle Expiatoire on the site of the Madeleine cemetery. Inside are two marble sculptures, *Marie Antoinette Praying at the Foot of Religion* and *Louis XVI Supported by an Angel*, and a painting by Alexandre Kucharski of the former queen in her cell. The Polish artist, dressed in a guard's uniform, allegedly snuck into the Conciergerie to paint the portrait. On each side of the path leading to the chapel are mass graves that hold the bodies of hundreds of Swiss Guards killed during the insurrection at the Tuileries on 10 August 1792.

OTHER PLACES

RIGHT BANK

PALAIS-ROYAL
Métro: Palais-Royal/Musée du Louvre

In 1780, this was the home of Louis XVI's cousin, the Duc de Chartres (the future Philippe Égalité), who commissioned three arcades to be built behind the palace. He rented the arcades as apartments, gambling houses, brothels, boutiques, and a wax museum. In 1782, one of the first great restaurants, La Grande Taverne de Londres, opened in the Palais-Royal; prior to this, meals were only served in inns or private homes. As royal property was not subject to police raids, the Palais-Royal quickly became popular with prostitutes and, in the late 1780s, political intrigue against the king was openly discussed in its many cafés. During the Revolution, the Palais-Royal was called the "the Liberty Pole of the city" as outside the popular Café de Foy (now Nos 57–60 Galerie de Montpensier), young activist Camille Desmoulins incited a crowd to storm the Bastille in July 1789.

Marie Antoinette visited the Palais-Royal many times as Dauphine and queen attending the opera, held here until 1781 when a fire destroyed the opera house. The Théâtre de Beaujolais (Nos 68–75 Galerie de Montpensier), now the Théâtre du Palais-Royal, was built in 1784 for marionette shows, and the Théâtre-Français, next to the western wing of the palace, was erected in 1786.

ROSE BERTIN'S SHOP
23, Rue de Richelieu ❈ *Métro: Palais-Royal/Musée du Louvre*

Marie Antoinette's favourite dressmaker, Rose Bertin, bought this property in 1789. Her last shop was located here in what is today the Passage Potier. She emigrated in 1792.

BANQUE DE FRANCE
48, Rue-Croix-des-Petits-Champs ❈ *Métro: Palais-Royal/Musée du Louvre*

This private palace was one of the homes of Marie Antoinette's close friend, the Princesse de Lamballe, and was owned by her father-in-law the Duc de Penthièvre, a descendant of Louis XIV. Upon his death in 1793, the hotel was declared national property.

SAINT-GERMAIN-L'AUXERROIS
2, Place du Louvre ❖ *Métro: Louvre*
In March 1790, Marie Antoinette's daughter took her first communion here at the parish church of the Tuileries.

BIBLIOTHÈQUE NATIONALE – RICHELIEU LIBRARY
58, Rue de Richelieu ❖ *Métro: Bourse*
Beginning in the 1600s, the royal library, which became the Bibliothèque Nationale, was housed here (although its headquarters have since moved to Quai François-Mauriac).

SQUARE DU TEMPLE
Rue du Temple, Rue de Bretagne, Rue Eugène-Spuller ❖ *Métro: Temple*
This park was the site of the Temple, a large complex belonging to Louis XVI's younger brother, the Comte d'Artois, which included a palatial mansion and a large tower, in which the royal family was imprisoned in 1792. Marie Antoinette's son, Louis-Charles, died in the tower on 8 June 1795. The tower was demolished in the early 1800s.

HÔTEL DE ROHAN
87, Rue Vieille-du-Temple ❖ *Métro: Rambuteau*
Built in 1705 by architect P.A. Delamair, the Cardinal de Rohan, from one of France's noblest families, lived in this mansion while embroiled in the Diamond Necklace Affair (1785). The famous *Salon des Singes*, in which the Cardinal entertained Madame de la Motte, still exists; this white and gold salon is decorated with lively monkeys playing the flute, teaching dogs to jump through hoops and other amusing human activities. This mansion is now part of the National Archives.

MUSÉE CARNAVALET
23, Rue de Sévigné ❖ *Métro: Saint-Paul*
The *Salle Louis XVI* in this museum dedicated to the history of Paris includes *Souvenirs de Marie Antoinette*.

HÔTEL DE VILLE
Place de l'Hôtel de Ville ❖ *Métro: Hôtel-de-Ville*

Known as the Place de Grève during the *Ancien Régime*, the market women gathered here before marching to Versailles in October 1789; Marie Antoinette and her family stopped at the city hall when they returned with the crowd to Paris. Marie Antoinette also visited it on her first visit to the city. Burned in May 1871, the city hall was rebuilt and looks similar to the original.

HÔTEL DE LA MARINE
2, Rue Royale ❖ *Métro: Concorde*

Built by Jacques-Ange Gabriel (1766-1775), the former royal Garde Meuble, (furniture warehouse) today houses the Ministry of the Marine. Gabriel also built the other colonnaded building on the northern side of the square; today it houses the Hôtel Crillon.

AXEL FERSEN'S RESIDENCE
27, Avenue Matignon (and 81, Rue du Faubourg Saint-Honoré) ❖ *Métro: Miromesnil*

In late 1789, after the royal family was forced to live in Paris, Axel Fersen, Marie Antoinette's confidante and supposed lover, moved into this mansion, which he used as his base while he planned the ill-fated escape of the royal family in 1791.

PARC MONCEAU
Main entrance: Boulevard de Courcelles ❖ *Métro: Monceau*

This lavish English garden, commissioned in 1778 by the Duc de Chartres (the future Philippe Égalité), was much admired by Marie Antoinette, who incorporated its design into gardens at the Petit Trianon. The Parc Monceau is filled with picturesque *folies* including a large colonnade, arch and pyramid. Paris once had 150 gardens with *folies*; now few remain, and this is the largest.

ROTONDE DE CHARTRES
Boulevard de Courcelles, at the entrance to the Parc Monceau ❖ *Métro: Monceau*

During Louis XVI's reign, a wall was erected around Paris with around 50 collection gates where taxes were paid on goods entering the city. Designed by Claude-Nicolas Ledoux, only four of these tiny neoclassical buildings survive. As symbols of royal taxation, many were burned down on 12 and 13 July 1789, just before the storming of the Bastille.

THÉÂTRE DE LA PORTE-SAINT-MARTIN
18, Boulevard Saint-Martin ❋ Métro: Strasbourg-Saint-Denis

Marie Antoinette commissioned this theatre, designed by Alexandre Lenoir, in 1781, and it was inaugurated with a free opera in honour of the birth of the Dauphin. During Louis XVI's reign, operas were performed here four times weekly, on Sundays, Tuesdays, Thursdays and Fridays. Opera balls, which began at midnight and closed at seven in the morning, were given here.

SITE OF THE BASTILLE
Place de la Bastille ❋ Métro: Bastille

On 14 July 1789, the citizens of Paris stormed the city's most hated monument: the prison of the Bastille. Originally built as a fortress, the Bastille became a symbol of royal oppression though it held only a handful of prisoners.

BOIS DE BOULOGNE
Métro: Les Sablons

One of Louis XVI's first acts as king was to open this enormous royal park to the public. The queen often visited on horseback or on foot, and people approached her personally with petitions. She attended horse races at a racecourse built by her brother-in-law, the Comte d'Artois, and her husband's cousin, the Duc de Chartres; these were the first horse races in Paris.

CHÂTEAU DE BAGATELLE
Bois de Boulogne, Parc de Bagatelle, Route de Sèvres à Neuilly ❋ Métro: Pont de Neuilly then bus 43 to Place de Bagatelle

"In the Bois de Boulogne, there is a country cottage called Bagatelle … which belongs to the Comte d'Artois… who discovered a very ingenious way of making sure that his expenses [for renovating it] were covered. He had a bet of 100,000 francs with the queen that this fairy palace would be started and finished during the court's journey to Fontainebleau." Louis Petit Bachaumont, *Mémoires secrets*, 22 October 1777.

In the autumn of 1777 Marie Antoinette impulsively bet her brother-in-law, the Comte d'Artois, that a château could not be constructed and furnished on his property in two months. The architect Bélanger hired 1,000 workmen who toiled night and day to complete construction. As there was a shortage of building materials, the king's younger brother ordered his guards to search the roads for carts of lime and plaster, and seize them even if they had already been sold. Although Bélanger paid for these materials, the original purchasers were furious. Against all odds, the architect completed the building in 50 days. The queen lost the bet and paid a vast sum to Artois. After visiting the château, try the adjacent *Les Jardins de Bagatelle* restaurant for an outdoor meal in the Parc de Bagatelle (www.restaurantbagatelle.com or call 01 40 67 98 29).

LEFT BANK

PETIT LUXEMBOURG
17, Rue de Vaugirard ❖ Métro: Luxembourg

The Petit Luxembourg, located west of the Luxembourg palace, was once the home to the Comte de Provence, Marie Antoinette's brother-in-law, and his wife until they emigrated, fleeing from France in June 1791. The government then quickly confiscated the property on behalf of the state. It is best seen from the Luxembourg gardens and now forms the official residence of the President of the Senate.

THÉÂTRE DE L'ODÉON
Place de l'Odéon ❖ Métro: Odéon

Marie Antoinette spent many happy nights in this theatre, then the largest in Paris and home of the Comédie-Française. She attended many plays here and particularly enjoyed the *Marriage of Figaro* by controversial author Beaumarchais. The theatre, built in 1780 on royal land near the Luxembourg, replaced an older Comédie-Française on the Rue de l'Ancienne Comédie. In 1799 and 1818, the building was renovated after fires.

PONT DE LA CONCORDE
Links the Place de la Concorde to the Left Bank ❖ Métro: Assemblée-Nationale; Concorde

This bridge, originally to be called Pont Louis XVI, was begun in 1788 and completed in 1791 (at the height of the French Revolution). It was built using stones taken from the Bastille.

PALAIS BOURBON (NATIONAL ASSEMBLY)
126-128, Rue de l'Université; 29-35, Quai d'Orsay ✳ *Métro: Assemblée-Nationale*

The Prince de Condé, the king's cousin, owned this palace; He emigrated three days after the fall of the Bastille and, in April 1792, the government confiscated this property.

LE CHAMP DE MARS
From the Seine to the École Militaire ✳ *Métro: École Militaire*

During the Revolution, the Champ des Mars was used for grand parades and on 14 July 1790, the Fête de la Fédération was held here to celebrate the first anniversary of the storming of the Bastille. Louis XVI and Marie Antoinette attended the outdoor festivities.

OUTSIDE PARIS

BASILIQUE DE SAINT-DENIS, SAINT-DENIS
1, Rue de la Légion d'Honneur ✳ *Métro: Basilique de Saint-Denis*

This Gothic basilica was the traditional cemetery of Bourbon kings. Marie Antoinette and Louis XVI's remains were brought here in 1815 and buried in the crypt. There are statues commemorating the royal couple, and an urn containing the heart of Louis XVII, little Louis-Charles, is kept in an underground chapel (la chapelle des Princes) in the crypt. Saint-Denis's neighbourhood can be rough, so visiting during daylight hours is suggested.

DOMAINE DE MONTREUIL - VERSAILLES (RÉSIDENCE DE MADAME ÉLISABETH)
73, Avenue de Paris

In 1783 Louis XVI purchased this home for his 18-year-old sister Elisabeth (1764-1794). Like Marie Antoinette, Elisabeth loved flowers and devoted much time to her elaborate garden and orangerie. Elisabeth rode in the carriage with the king and queen when they left Versailles for Paris on 6 October 1789 and, as they passed her home, she leaned forward and bade it goodbye. Marie Antoinette wrote her last letter to Elisabeth, who shared her imprisonment at the Temple and was guillotined in May 1794. Montreuil is a 20-minute walk from the château.

HÔTEL DES MENUS PLAISIRS - VERSAILLES
22, Avenue de Paris

The first session of the Estates General met in the former *salle des Menus plaisirs* (Hall of Lesser Pleasures) near the château. Louis XVI selected this hall, originally used to hold stage scenery and props, for the sessions, and it was quickly decorated with faux columns and painted white and gold. This building now houses the Centre for Baroque Music.

CHÂTEAU ET PARC DE CHANTILLY - CHANTILLY
MUSÉE CONDÉ AND LE HAMEAU

Marie Antoinette built her *hameau* at the Trianon after seeing the one built at Chantilly, the ancestral home of the Prince de Condé. Built in 1774, the fairytale village can be visited, and there is a nearby café for refreshments including gingerbread with crème Chantilly (sweetened whipped crème, which was invented here). Inside the château, home of the Musée Condé, is François-Hubert Drouais's portrait of Marie Antoinette as Hebe, as well as several of Louis XVI and his brothers. Chantilly is a 30-minute train ride from Paris departing from the Gare du Nord.

MUSÉE NATIONAL DE CÉRAMIQUE DE SÈVRES - SÈVRES
Place de la manufacture, 92310 Sèvres ❈ *Métro: Pont de Sèvres*

In 1759, Louis XV became the financial backer of the Sèvres manufactory, which made luxury porcelain for the royal family and aristocracy. Their china museum, exhibits an extensive collection of hard-paste and soft-paste porcelain made for the Bourbons and the court, including several pieces that belonged to Madame du Barry.

DOMAINE NATIONAL DE SAINT-CLOUD - SAINT-CLOUD
92210 Saint-Cloud ❈ *Métro: Pont de Saint-Cloud*

In 1784 Louis XVI bought the château de Saint-Cloud which overlooked the Seine from his cousin, the Duc d'Orléans, for Marie Antoinette. The deeds were in her name and, as at the Trianon, she personally issued orders. This summer palace became one of her favourite homes, but the huge expenditure, which came as France faced tremendous financial difficulty, only increased the queen's unpopularity. One politician remarked, "It is equally impolitic and immoral to see palaces belonging to a Queen of France." The château burned down in 1870. All that remains are the park and the famous fountains called the "Grand Cascade".

BREGUET

20, Place Vendôme ✦ *www.breguet.com* ✦ *Métro: Madeleine, Opera*

Breguet, one of the world's great watchmakers, was founded in 1775 by Swiss-born Abraham-Louis Breguet (1747–1823), an inventive horologist legendary for his knowledge of mechanics. This horological genius created many unusual timepieces including the automatic or *perpétuelle* watch, which became popular in 1780. In October 1782, he made a self-winding *perpétuelle* watch with a date indication for Marie Antoinette, who became so attached to the thin gold repeater that she ordered several as gifts. An officer of her Guard commissioned another watch for her and requested that Breguet add as many technological advances as possible. The watchmaker was not able to complete this item before the Revolution.

Breguet lived at 39, Quai de l'Horloge near the Pont Neuf on the Île de la Cité. During the late 1700s, this was Paris's clock making district, and his workshop, which employed a hundred men, was located there. This company's heritage includes many royal patrons including Louis XVI and his cousin the Duc d'Orléans, Napoleon took three of Breguet's timepieces on his Egyptian campaign in 1798, and other clients included the Austrian royal family and Tsar Alexander I. In 1810, Breguet invented the world's first wristwatch for Napoleon's younger sister, Queen Caroline of Naples. Now located in the Place Vendôme, Breguet has a small museum under the boutique that displays historic watches and clocks; it's open to the public, but you must call at least a day ahead to make an appointment.

MELLERIO DITS MELLER
9, Rue de la Paix ❋ *www.mellerio.com* ❋ *Métro: Madeleine, Opera*

Jean Mellerio was unwittingly in the right place at the right time when Marie Antoinette noticed him selling goods to nobles near the château of Versailles. Impressed by the enterprising young jeweller, the queen arranged for him to become a vendor on the palace grounds. During the *Ancien Régime*, vendors filled Versailles' courtyards and outer rooms, and even the royal family bought items from these salespeople.

Fourteen generations of the Mellerio family have operated Mellerio dits Meller since the legendary jeweller was founded in 1613. Mellerio is the oldest jeweller in Paris and has conducted business at this location since 1815. Prior to that, the famous jewellers were located on the Rue Vivienne near the Palais-Royal. Originally an Italian family, the Mellerios emigrated to Paris and began providing jewellery to French royalty in the seventeenth century. Empress Josephine, who patronized many of Marie Antoinette's purveyors, became a frequent customer in the 1800s, as did many of the Bonapartes. Today François Mellerio runs the company.

ANCIENNE MANUFACTURE ROYALE
11, Rue Royale (in the Bernadaud boutique) ❋ *www.manufacture-royale.com* ❋ *Métro: Madeleine, Concorde*

The Ancienne Manufacture Royale (Former Royal Manufacturer), founded in 1737, became part of the royal Sèvres porcelain workshops under the protection of Louis XVI in 1784. Two years earlier, Sèvres had delivered an exquisite service to Marie Antoinette decorated with pearls, her favourite jewellery, set against a vivid green background. The porcelain was adorned with delicate cornflowers, in a shade of blue that exactly matched the queen's eyes. Royale sells the identical pattern today, as well as several pieces from the *Service de la Laiterie de Rambouillet*. This dairy service, made by the Sèvres manufactory in 1787, included a cup used for drinking milk; shaped like a woman's breast, it rested on a tripod of goat heads. Several other brightly coloured porcelain cups and saucers adorned with goats or cows from the Rambouillet service are available. All are identical reproductions of the queen's china; the originals are housed in the National Ceramics Museum at Sèvres [see Other Places, page 156]. Royale's popular "historical cups" series features designs from the 1770s and 1780s, including *Aux Dauphins* created to celebrate the birth of Marie Antoinette's first son in 1781. This was the first company to mark their products as "Limoges".

ODIOT

7, Place de la Madeleine ❧ *www.odiot.com* ❧ *Métro: Madeleine*

In the late 1700s, Jean-Baptiste Claude Odiot was a prominent goldsmith whose shop was "At the sign of the Cross of Gold" on the Rue Saint-Honoré near the Church of Saint-Roch. He was friends with Thomas Jefferson, then the American ambassador to France, and executed, after Jefferson's design, a silver *fontaine* (tea or coffee urn) and pair of silver christening cups. Odiot is one of the oldest goldsmiths in France.

PRELLE

5, Place des Victoires ❧ *www.prelle.com* ❧ *Métro: Bourse, Palais-Royal/Musée du Louvre*

Maison Prelle of Lyons has been manufacturing magnificent hand-woven luxury textiles since 1752. Their silks have decorated rooms and furniture at the royal residences of Fontainebleau, the Tuileries, Saint-Cloud and the Élysee palace. They wove the sumptuous summer wall coverings now seen in Marie Antoinette's bedchamber at the château of Versailles as well as fabrics for her boudoir and theatre at the Petit Trianon. Dozens of patterns dating from the eighteenth century can be ordered from their showroom or viewed on their website including *Chevaux de la Reine*, a fabric created to match Marie Antoinette's hair. Among the exquisite reissues from their extensive historic archive is a blue grey fabric with white and pink flowers taken from a design of Madame Eloffe, *modiste* to Marie Antoinette, and a crème *velour* with dark green garlands made for Madame du Barry's library at Versailles.

HÔTEL ROYAL SAINT-HONORÉ

221, Rue Saint-Honoré ❧ *www.hotel-royal-st-honore.com* ❧ *Métro: Tuileries*

On the southwest corner of Rue Saint-Honoré and Rue d'Alger, the Hôtel de Noailles, built in 1687, served as the Marquis de La Fayette's Parisian residence. In 1774, he married the young Mademoiselle Noailles, from one of France's wealthiest families; this mansion, near the Place Vendôme, belonged to her family and La Fayette lived here while in the capital. On 15 February 1779, Marie Antoinette stopped here to greet La Fayette upon his return to France from fighting in America.

HÔTEL WASHINGTON OPÉRA

50, Rue de Richelieu ❧ *www.hotelwashingtonopera.com* ❧ *Métro: Palais-Royal*

A block from the Palais-Royal, this hotel was once the Paris townhouse of the Marquise de Pompadour, Louis XV's mistress legendary for her elegant taste.

LEFT BANK

DEBAUVE & GALLAIS

30, Rue des Saints-Pères ✵ *www.debauve-et-gallais.com* ✵ *Métro: Saint Germain des Pres*

Official supplier to kings of France and winner of countless awards, Debauve & Gallais still make their famous chocolate *Pistoles de Marie Antoinette*, from the same recipe created over two hundred years ago for the queen. Sulpice Debauve, who then served as chemist to the royal family, concocted the novel combination of cocoa, cane sugar, and medicine after Marie Antoinette complained to him about the unpleasant taste of the medicines she had to take. Tradition has it that the queen herself originated the sweet's name when she first saw the small coin-shaped chocolates displayed on a tray. Although they no longer contain medicine, the *pistoles* are still made in several varieties; Marie Antoinette preferred the almond milk flavour. In Vienna, she grew up drinking hot chocolate for breakfast and continued to do so after arriving in France. Debauve supplied a hot chocolate flavoured with cinnamon and coffee for the queen. It was brought to her each morning in a porcelain *chocolatière* with a wooden handle. Debauve & Gallais's luxurious boutique on the Rue des Saint-Pères dates to 1819 and is classified as a historical monument. Built as a chocolate pharmacy, it serves as a reminder that, in the eighteenth century, chocolate was considered to have healing benefits and was used for headaches, as an analgesic and to ease muscle spasms. There is also a Right Bank branch at 33, Rue Vivienne (Métro: Bourse; call 01 40 39 05 50) near the Palais-Royal.